The Chef's Commandments: Maximize Your Kitchen's Profitability

Building and Maintaining a Successful, Profit-Driven Restaurant

Author: J.A. Mendez
Editor: C. Pinheiro

Pineapple Publications
Elk Grove, CA

A special thanks to Jami and Tom Herman, Collette Szymborski and Brandon O'Dell

www.thechefscommandments.com

ISBN: 0982266022
EAN-13: 9780982266021

Author: J.A. Mendez
Editor: C. Pinheiro

www.pineapplepublications.com

Coming Soon:
The Chef's Commandments
Series!

Book #1
ISBN: 0982266022
Maximize Your Kitchen's Profitability:
Building and Maintaining a Successful, Profit-Driven Restaurant

Book #2
ISBN: 0982266030
Happy Cooks, Happy Customers
A Chef's Guide to Employee Management
Staffing, Hiring, Recruiting, Disciplining, and Training Guide for Restaurants

Book #3 (coming soon)
A Chef's Guide to Restaurant Marketing, Promotion, Publicity, and Financial Wellness

Book #4 (coming soon)
Controlling Costs:
Inventory Management, Food Costing Techniques, and Profitable Menu Practices

Book #5 (coming soon)
Perfect Sanitation: the Ideal Model for Restaurant Cleanliness and Food Safety

Table of Contents

"Don't be afraid to make mistakes, everyone does, but only those that admit their responsibility in the mistake learn from it. Those are the people that can keep trying and eventually taste success."

-Brandon O'Dell, O'Dell Restaurant Consulting

Introduction

A chef wears many hats. As a chef, you will be asked to do all the regular tasks that a manager would do, including training and firing employees, performance appraisals, and sometimes even deal with unhappy guests. But your job is greater than that of a regular manager. You have the power to make or break a restaurant. You are the **leader** in the kitchen—its chef.

You must have a commitment to service, food quality, and still be able to monitor costs. This means that you have to be a chef, a businessperson, and a director. Chefs have multiple layers of responsibility—to the guest, to the employees, and to the business itself. The degree to which you can control all of these unique responsibilities will be the defining factor in your ultimate success. It's a balancing act—and a bit of planning and some common sense can go a long way to saving you thousands of dollars every year.

On a typical day, 44 percent of all the adults in the United States eat at a restaurant. With all of this profit potential, why do so many restaurants still fail?

According to recent studies from Cornell and Ohio State Universities, 59-60 percent of restaurants fail within the first three years, with as many as seventy-five percent failing within the first five. The failure rate for restaurants is high.

You must learn how to think like a businessperson. This means that your responsibilities will go beyond cooking and supervision. Develop a plan for your restaurant to succeed. The key to having a successful, profit-driven kitchen is learning how to mitigate **all** your costs and still produce a happy customer. A restaurant's success is not measured only in customer satisfaction—the harsh reality is that a restaurant can have a very satisfied customer base and still be drowning financially.

The best chefs recognize potential problems *before* they occur. Successful chefs also recognize when their business model needs an adjustment.

Just like any other business, restaurants have assets and liabilities that must be protected. Your assets include obvious things like equipment, cash, and inventory, but employees are also assets that must be monitored, promoted, and reprimanded as necessary.

This book is designed to be a beginning guide and overview for chefs, kitchen managers, and culinary beginners who are looking for direction on how to cut costs and manage waste while still producing a quality product for their customers. This is the first book in our series on restaurant profitability. In this book, you will learn how to:

1. Manage food inventories, cut food costs, and reduce food waste.
2. Stretch your marketing dollar!
3. Create a more profitable menu.
4. Eliminate employee accidents.
5. Stop employee theft!
6. Strive for perfect sanitation.
7. Cut labor costs and reduce employee turnover.
8. Introduce special menus.
9. Increase perceived value.
10. Increase revenue by catering, and by hosting special events and parties.

Commandment #1: Control Food Costs and Reduce Waste

"The allowable level for waste is zero."

-**Ken Burgin**, director of Profitable Hospitality

Control Food Costs and Reduce Waste

Restaurants fail and succeed just like any other business. The largest cost by far in most kitchens is **food**. The National Restaurant Association estimates that twenty percent of all food prepared commercially in the United States goes into the trash.[1] Food costs are a consistent problem in every restaurant.

Food cost can be calculated as follows:
Food Cost = Cost of Food Sales / Food Sales.

Generally, waste reduction and good inventory practices **immediately** produce cost savings. Food costs must be tracked weekly. Costs should stay between 25-30 percent depending on the type of restaurant. Steakhouses typically have a higher food cost at about 35 percent.

Although food costs may be the same, fine dining establishments have a lower profit margin because of higher labor costs. Profits are lower in full-service restaurants. Profits are higher in cafeterias and casual dining establishments. The determining factor in this case is usually labor cost. In a casual dining restaurant, if overhead and labor are tracked diligently, the profit margins can be as high as 25 percent. This goes up even higher if the owner and the owner's family provides significant labor or other services. This is easier is "mom and pop" restaurants where everyone in the family typically helps out.

Track food costs over a specific period and watch the spikes and downturns. Typically, restaurants track food costs over a twenty-eight day period. Some restaurants track their food costs quarterly, but if you are just starting out, you need to

---

[1] National Restaurant Association statistical analysis, www.restaurant.org

monitor your food costs more frequently than just once every quarter.

Juices, coffee, sodas, and other non-alcoholic beverage sales are usually included in food cost calculations. Alcohol is always tracked and calculated separately, with the exception of cooking wine and other alcohol that is used exclusively in the kitchen and not for serving to customers.

1. Take an Accurate Food Inventory

An accurate inventory is the most important part of managing restaurant food cost. If you don't take the time to do this correctly, your restaurant will almost certainly be doomed to failure. Nobody likes getting up at 5 a.m. to do inventory, but the most successful restaurants do weekly inventories and keep accurate par levels. When I see a restaurant with outrageous food costs, I can usually trace the problem back to a sloppy food inventory and to over-portioning. The ***first step*** for a successful, profit-driven kitchen is an accurate food inventory. If you are sloppy about your inventory practices, your cooks will be sloppy about theirs, too.

You must learn to adjust your par levels for special events, such as holidays or parties. Certain holidays like Mother's Day, Father's Day, and Secretaries Day are all big revenue days. Par levels must be adjusted for these days and also for any local events that might bring in more customers.

A good inventory discovers waste, employee theft (did you only sell twenty rib-eyes this week, but fifty rib-eyes are missing?), and food spoilage. The Executive Chef or Sous Chef should always perform the weekly inventory and par levels.

Another good tip is to remove anything that might "disguise" food losses. Do your servers have an "*open food*" key? Do your bartenders have an "*open liquor*" key on their register? Get RID of it! This is one of the first places servers and bartenders will go to steal, or else these become a catch-all for miscellaneous items that you will never be able to track.

As much as you want to assume the best in people, experience teaches that anyone can succumb to dishonesty if faced with various difficulties. This includes the use of an *"open food"* key to mask giveaways and other skimming techniques commonly used by servers and bartenders.

2. Make Strategic Food Orders

The second step in a profit-driven kitchen is accurate food orders. Food orders should be adjusted every week and should agree with predetermined par levels. Make adjustments for special events, holidays, and local variables such as a concert or festival.

If you have multiple suppliers, do comparative shopping to see who will give you the best price and food quality. There are some stories in the industry about vindictive suppliers that discontinue service when chefs try to price shop. So take this into account when searching for the best price. You may also want to consider negotiating an exclusive contract with one supplier; sometimes this allows you to obtain lower prices across the board. Check your supplier's price sheets weekly. Get a staff member to do this. If you see a price that is higher than the price that you were quoted, request a credit memo.

Always order in a timely manner, but do not order too early because this will lead to spoilage and waste. "Standing" food orders are for lazy chefs. Do not use a standing order unless absolutely necessary, such as when you are on vacation. Always do your weekly food order from scratch, and adjust pars as necessary. You can order more of non-perishable items, such as dry goods, but always control the inventory of perishable items religiously if you want to succeed.

All food orders should be done actually *standing in* the dry storage and the walk-in, not while sitting in a cozy back office. Make sure that you can actually see the food you need. Touch the boxes and verify the cases. Busy cooks are notorious for taking small amounts of product out of storage and leaving the boxes on the shelf as if they were full.

Also, adjust food quality requirements based on common sense needs. You don't need to purchase Grade A apples just to make applesauce! Don't purchase fancy almonds just to slice them up for salads. You get the idea. Adjust food orders based on your restaurant's current needs. You can save money without skimping on food quality if you order intelligently.

Monitor supply and demand on your raw goods. Watch out for volatile food costs (another reason never to have a "standing food order"). Many food items have high fluctuations in price. Did a natural disaster just wipe out the Haas avocado crop? Can you switch to another variety? You can save a lot of money looking for good substitutions for expensive or out-of-season products.

If possible, use substitutions rather than purchasing from the supermarket. Try to develop friendly relationships with other restaurant owners. They may be able to help you in a pinch. We frequently "borrow" items from our neighboring restaurants. They also contact us when they need help. A case of romaine lettuce costs $24, but in the supermarket, each individual head of lettuce is $2. Can you borrow a case from your neighbor? Maybe half a case will get you through dinner, and you can return the case to your neighbor after your next delivery date. Good chefs help each other to be successful. Develop relationships with other restaurants. This can be a good thing for both parties.

Remember: Supermarket Purchasing is a Curse!

Unless an item is wildly popular, consider discontinuing it if the food cost is too high, or if the ingredients are highly perishable. Even if an item has a low food cost, if you are throwing away the ingredients every week, or purchasing odd ingredients at the supermarket, then the plate's "hidden costs" might actually make it an unprofitable menu selection. Certain items, like edible flowers, are extremely perishable and can cause your food costs to skyrocket.

Chefs like to use exotic items, because it gives them a chance to show off their expertise. Just make sure you aren't throwing your profits in the dumpster because you want to have more exotic-looking dishes.

One of the most expensive items restaurants purchase is meat. If possible, purchase meat in bulk. Train employees how to cut and trim meat and fish. This leaves you less dependent on pre-cut items, which are always higher priced. If possible, invest in a larger cold storage space so you can purchase whole sides of beef. Whole fish is always cheaper than fillet. A cook who is a good fish cutter can save you thousands of dollars per year by allowing you to purchase whole fish.

3. Eagle-Eye Receiving

Make sure that a manager always inspects the food order when it is received. Inspect goods for weight, quality, and accurate counts. The chef should personally schedule and receive food and beverage deliveries. Claims for damaged goods must be noted at the time of delivery—suppliers often will not take back damaged or spoiled goods if you discover them later.

If any goods are missing or damaged, get a credit memo or notation from the delivery driver. With seafood, or other super-premium items such as steaks, missing cases or partially spoiled food can cost thousands of dollars on just one delivery.

Have probe thermometers and a dedicated scale in the delivery area so that you can check item temperatures and weights. Non-conforming items can be identified and returned immediately. Once again, a case of warm lobsters can cost hundreds of dollars. Make sure you always temperature check and weigh your premium items.

Every single delivery should be monitored. **Do not** accept food deliveries during your busy periods. Have your delivery times listed conspicuously on the back door. Make sure a manager is always present to accept large deliveries. This is extremely important!

4. Neat Food Storage

Clean, neat food storage is also essential to controlling food costs. The dry storage must be orderly, with items off the floor, away from dirt or moisture. Invest in good shelving units in order to keep your expensive dry goods away from the floor (used shelves are usually okay.) Remember, less product on the shelf equals more money in your pocket, so keeping your shelves neat allows you to track food turnover and inventory better.

Make sure the shelves are labeled, or otherwise clearly marked. All items should be dated, and rotated frequently. If you have to spend ten minutes looking for a ladle or a packet of spices, you aren't using your time wisely. Plan your dry storage to be efficient and food-saving. Organization saves money.

All items should be stored at the correct temperature. Use the "first in-first out" procedure, which says that the oldest product should always be used first. Shelf labels and food stickers (Day Dots) are cheap and well worth the price. There's no excuse for not rotating stock or putting food items in the right place.

Don't keep expensive items in your regular dry storage. Saffron, caviar, truffles, and other luxury foods should be treated like cash. Always keep these items locked in a safe or in your office. If the items are perishable, invest in a cage for your walk-in. Lobsters, ribs, and filet mignon are all examples of items that should be kept locked.

5. Use Everything!

Avoid food waste. If practicable, use steak trimmings for stock pots and other recipes. Try to throw away as little as possible. Try to avoid throwing away food because of spoilage by turning over inventory quickly. **Never serve spoiled food!** A single lawsuit from food-borne illness can erase all your careful savings in an instant.

Make sure your cooks have accurate recipe cards and prep sheets with photos. Using recipe cards helps the cooks, and it helps your menu items to be dependable. Cards help reduce waste and confusion, especially when your restaurant is new, or you decide to switch menu items. Customers love a reliable product, and one of the bigger mistakes that inexperienced chefs make is to prepare dishes without using a consistent recipe.

An old restaurant trick is to use older food items to prepare a nightly special. This prevents spoilage of good product and keeps you from wasting inventory. If you have excess food, donate it to a food bank or homeless shelter. Never give excess food to the staff, even at the end of the night. This creates a culture of "giving away" food to employees, and it is a difficult practice to break.

6. Watch Portion Sizes!

Portion control, portion control, portion control—the mantra of every successful chef! Portion control is not just about watching how much wasted food goes into the garbage—it's also about learning how to plate food creatively. Good presentation can disguise smaller portion sizes. This is why restaurants use lettuce leaves and kale under appetizer dishes—it creates the illusion of a larger portion for very little cost.

Using smaller plates creates the illusion of a larger portion. Also, serving soup with a saucer or plate underneath makes the soup bowl appear larger. The presentation is better, and the customer believes they are receiving a larger amount of food.

Institute the use of portion bags. This small change can save thousands of dollars each month. The employees may grumble, but the use of portion bags always saves money. The labor costs associated with portioning food is worth the savings when portion bag systems are used.

For example, in restaurants that use a lot of dairy, using portion bags for shredded cheese can save hundreds of dollars every month. Over-portioning is a subtle but significant source of food waste, and tends to happen more at peak hours when the restaurant is busy and cooks don't have the time or inclination to measure food out properly.

Over-portioning can result in huge losses over time, especially with higher-cost items, such as steak or chicken. For example, let's take a higher-priced item like Ahi tuna. At $12 per pound, an over-portion of just a quarter of an ounce adds a cost of 33 cents to a six-ounce dinner portion. This doesn't seem like much, right? If your kitchen serves twenty-five plates of Ahi per day, that's a loss of $3,000 per year. Imagine the losses on an even higher-priced item!

Exact portions and weights should always be used for premium items such as fish, steak, chicken, and shellfish. The savings can be enormous over time. Save odd-sized pieces and use them in other things such as a weekly special or lunch special.

Another important area for cost savings is the fryers. Fry oil is a big expense in many restaurants, so you need to reduce costs by cutting fry oil waste. Always rotate the fryers. Designate one fryer for "crumbly" food, such as floured or breaded foods. Flaky foods break down the oil faster, so designating one fryer for these items allows you to change the oil in all the fryers less frequently.

Use a test kit in order to verify when the fryer oil should be changed. Don't ever change the oil on an assigned schedule (like every Tuesday). Only change the fryer oil when the test kit indicates that it should be changed. Run fryers at a lower temperature—they don't have to be set to the highest setting. This saves energy and keeps the fryer oil from breaking down so fast.

Don't turn on the fryers in the morning. Wait until you open your doors. The fryers generally take about ten minutes to heat up, so this is generally enough time to allow the oil to heat up. Some restaurants don't turn on the fryers until they get their first fried food order. If you don't sell much fried food, you may want to consider this energy saving tip. This also extends the life of your oil and saves energy.

Make sure the barrels of waste oil are covered outside; this prevents water from entering the oil, which can make it unsalable. Sell waste oil and cardboard for additional income.

Make sure that cooks have all the tools they need to succeed. The kitchen should have digital scales for measuring product, and appropriately-sized ladles, cups, and other measuring implements. Servers are notorious for over-serving food, such as salad dressings and ice cream. Make sure the servers know you are serious about food costs. Point out the correct portion sizes for dressings, ice cream, and other commonly over-portioned foods.

Take out the Trash (Cans!)

Another tip to reduce food waste is to completely remove all the trash cans from the kitchen area. Instead, use clear bins and make sure that each employee (especially in the prep area) has his/her own bin to throw waste and trimmings. At the end of each shift, (or periodically) go through the bins and review the amount of waste. Use this as an opportunity to congratulate employees for doing a good job, and also to train employees on the importance of watching food costs.

Owners can use a morale booster like a gift card or a gas card to the cook who saves the most food by the end of the week! This method has been shown to lower food costs by up to 5 percent over time. It provides employees with "psychological encouragement" to reduce food waste.

7. Employee Incentives and Training

Employee incentives are a significant component of a safety and waste reduction program, and all employees from managers to the clean-up crew should be included. Training should be repeated periodically to ensure that new employees are included. An employee suggestion and awards program can be established to maintain enthusiasm for the program.[2]

When implementing a new program, consider giving the cooks an incentive for meeting kitchen food cost targets by offering them a bonus if they do. You can recognize one cook as the "food cost leader" for the month. The extra recognition is free and boosts morale.

Although it is alright to point out incorrect procedure, do not openly rebuke or belittle an employee in front of other

[2] Ibid #1

employees. But it is always okay to point out when an employee is doing an excellent job! Sometimes vocal praise of one employee who is doing things well is more effective than pointing out when someone else is doing things wrong.

Gas cards or gift cards are highly coveted and often work better than cash. The food cost savings offset the amount of employee bonuses, and it shows goodwill toward your most valuable employees. The main factors in the successful management of food costs are diligence and hard work. Make sure all the employees understand how important food cost is to the restaurant's success.

8. Implement a Waste Reduction Program

Many restaurants have been very successful with waste reduction, and so yours can be too. Once a restaurant has made a commitment to reduce waste, the chef or kitchen manager should assess all operations such as food preparation, food service, purchasing, and even janitorial activities to identify opportunities to reduce waste and conserve water, food, and electricity. All of these techniques result in cost savings. The benefits of a waste-reduction program include:

1. Cutting costs or generating revenue.
2. Enhancing your corporate image.
3. Increasing your employee morale.
4. Making a positive impact on the environment.[3]

These are some options for food waste reduction:

- Order bulk supplies.

---

[3] Full Circle Resources, "Bridging the Gap," Missouri Department of Natural Resources.

- Terminate useless packaging from the vendor, reducing shipping costs.
- Purchase reusable items. Purchase durable items such as air hand dryers that are designed to reduce waste.
- Purchase only the minimum amount of raw goods needed for a set period of time. This practice will help eliminate out-of-date products and excess goods.
- Clearly label all materials. Labels should indicate contents, storage and handling, and expiration dates.[4]

Innovative Waste Reduction

Some chefs have gone to great lengths to reduce waste. According to KLS TV, Sean Wharton, owner of The Gateway Grill in Kamas, has decided to save all of his food waste and feed it to— his pigs![5]

Wharton got tired of seeing all the trimmings and table scraps go to waste, so he trained all of his employees to throw food waste into a "pig bucket". He takes the food home and feeds it to his pigs, which he then sells to willing buyers. He has sold dozens of pigs already, and has even inspired other restaurants to do the same.

---

4 North Carolina Department of Environment and Natural Resources. October 1999. *A Fact Sheet for Managing Food Materials.*

5 Restaurant owner finds new way to recycle food waste, KSL TV Utah

According to Recycle Utah, there are at least 10 restaurants that are now following suit.

Wharton saves on garbage costs, too. He estimates that he is saving $250 a month on dumping fees alone, not to mention the reduction in flies, bugs, and other pests that are primarily attracted to food garbage.

Can you think of innovative ways to reduce waste and increase your profits at the same time? Sean Wharton did—and so can you!

Interview with the Financial Expert

Collette Szymborski, CPA
Elk Grove Accountancy Corporation
Certified Public Accountant
Managing Partner
www.elkgrovecpa.com

What do you think is the main reason why restaurants have such a high failure rate?

Collette: There are a number of reasons. In the restaurant business, typically you have an owner who has put in a lot of time working in the industry, either as a chef or a server, but they might not have the education or the business skills to understand how to really run a restaurant. You can be the best chef in the world, but if you don't know how to budget and manage your costs, you *will* get into trouble.

Do feel like the major issues with restaurant failure are labor costs or food costs? What do you feel is the deciding factor?

Collette: Most of the failures happen with the "mom and pop" restaurants. A person who puts their entire life savings into a dream—they dump everything they have into a new undertaking, and the money just isn't enough to keep the business afloat while they build up the clientele.

Franchises are different. Typically, a franchise restaurant has a higher success rate because of the name recognition. But there's a big hurdle to get into a franchise to begin with.

Many people who start new restaurants never really think through the costs that it takes to start up. The equipment, the staff training, and the advertising—it all adds up, and costs just get away from them.

New chefs generally UNDER-estimate their costs, and OVER-estimate their revenues. They just don't have the cash flow. Once a restaurant has been around for a while (typically three years), they can fine-tune their profitability. Most people are not good at being **everything.**

It's hard to be a cook, manager, bookkeeper, and everything else. No one can wear so many hats. This is where the smaller start-ups get into trouble.

Theft is a huge problem in this industry…

Collette: Yes, bars especially. The owner doesn't want to stay around until 2 a.m., so they hire someone, and that's when the theft takes place. The owner can't be everywhere at once. Some of these issues can be mitigated, but it's very difficult to stop all theft all the time.

Theft is not going to bankrupt the business, though. Theft will minimize a restaurant's profit, but it generally won't break them unless the theft is egregious.

So what about the "controls" issue?

Collette: You won't have a real problem with theft UNLESS you have someone who has way more control than they need to. This is the "separation of duties" that accountants talk about all the time. If the owner is running the restaurant, he or she should be totally involved in all the cash handling—and all the cash duties MUST be segregated.

If a single employee is going to the bank, and also reviewing the register tape, and also doing the reconciliations, you have a situation where it is really easy for someone to steal and also cover their tracks. Owners have to segregate duties, or else the owner is the one who should physically do the bank drop. The owner should be the one reviewing the bank statement every month. An owner that is not involved to that degree leaves himself open for theft.

If you give a staff member the authority over all the cash, then your restaurant is an easy target for an unscrupulous employee. And it's usually a manager, or a bookkeeper. But it can happen all the way down the line, down to the dishwasher taking home food and silverware.

If you aren't aware of where your money is going, you are going to have serious problems down the road.

So what do you recommend that owners do?

Collette: Well, make sure that you have oversight over everything. Even if you give other staff members the authority to manage the cash, but you do cash drops and till audits, then you can protect yourself. The more you involve yourself in the day-to-day cash activities, the less likely your employees will steal—because they will be afraid to get caught.

Change cash drawers in the middle of a shift. And don't get lazy after you start doing well. This is what a lot of owners do. They start to trust their staff, and they think everything is going to be okay, but often this is not the case.

Before I became a CPA, I worked in a restaurant. The restaurant was long-established—thirty years in the same location. They had the same bookkeeper for fifteen years. She developed a drug problem, and she started stealing. It didn't destroy the restaurant, the restaurant continued after the bookkeeper was fired, but who knows how much that bookkeeper stole? And it broke the owner's heart because the bookkeeper was like family.

And the owners terminated her?

Collette: Yes, they terminated her **and** had her convicted for theft! If you allow one person in your business to steal, you've pretty much given free reign to any other employee that wants to do the same. Theft won't destroy a business, but it will definitely hurt.

So what do you think really destroys a new restaurant?

Collette: Well, behaviors, mostly. And not having enough capital at the beginning to keep you going. Owners need to be realistic about their sales. They need to find their break even point. You have to assume that your costs are going to be high and your revenues are going to be low, especially at the beginning.

You can't force customers to come in and eat. You can spend $10,000 in advertising, but that's still no guarantee that the advertising is going to generate new customers. The real success stories are owners that do a lot of the work at the beginning, and really pinch their pennies until they get over those lean years.

If you don't have the capital, you're better off getting a taco truck (*laughter*).

So you really tell clients that they should go out and get a taco truck?

Collette: Well, yes—it's a joke, but the theory is accurate—start out small if you can't afford a real place of business. See if you can make it catering out of your home, as a personal chef, or with a "taco truck." If you can do this, and you save up enough capital, *then* open up your dream restaurant.

So you're saying that people really do need to have competent financial advice.

Collette: Well—the economy is bad. No one is an expert in *everything*. I really recommend that business owners talk to a financial adviser, such as a CPA. And *listen* to them. It doesn't mean you're a failure. You're a success if you surround yourself with people that can help you. Don't hide your head in the sand.

Unless you have an accounting background, you need to find someone who can assist you with your financial affairs. And you need to be able to *take* that advice; otherwise you're just wasting your money.

Do you have any pointers for a new chef?

Collette: The time to change behavior is BEFORE the problem gets too big to manage. If you are struggling, it's time to step back and look at what you can do to change your situation. Your financial adviser should be objective. My job is to help you change your behavior so you can be more successful. That's what I get paid to do. A lot of that has to do with changing bad habits.

What do you mean by "bad habits?"

Collette: Well, I mean people who draw money out of the business without being able to afford it. Business owners have to learn how to budget their cash. It always comes back to cash flow. If you feel like you're money-starved and you have a good month, owners always want to pull all that money out. It's a big mistake. It's always better to take a consistent draw that's *reasonable*, and affordable. After you've become established, you can increase your draws, but even then it should be done gradually.

It takes a lot of discipline to be successful. And not everyone has that.

How often do you come in when the business is already failing?

Collette: More often than I'd like. Sometimes, things are beyond salvation. Sometimes big problems occur when you have too many cooks in the kitchen. Often, problems arise when you have multiple owners. You have four people running a business together and they don't like each other anymore. And you really can't fix that. These are failed partnerships and failed relationships. This is usually due to unreasonable expectations or lack of communication. A business failure is like an expensive divorce.

Restaurants are cyclical by nature. If you are going to run a business, you have to be proficient at managing your money and also managing your staff.

It's just like running a household, but on a much larger scale. Your staff might be like family, but you can't afford to pay them to do nothing. So send them home. Do the work yourself. This goes back to managing your labor dollars. It's all outflows and inflows. You can only keep what you can afford, and you shouldn't buy more than you can use.

For the restaurants that have been successful, what do you feel that the owners have done differently? What do you find in successful restaurants that you don't find in unsuccessful ones?

Well, successful restaurants have regular customers! [laughter] If a restaurant can make it past the first three years, they're usually home free. If a restaurant fails *after* those first three years, it's usually a catastrophe—the owner has died, or it's a divorce, it's a major issue.

Most restaurants that fail actually fail in the first year, because they didn't have enough capital to open in the first place. And the food and service may have been *wonderful.* But they just weren't around long enough to get those customers to come back and become regulars.

People are very faithful to what they like. I remember a wonderful little dessert place that opened up downtown—the best desserts I'd ever had in my whole life! I was so excited, and I was talking to my husband about going back. So, sixty days later, I go back to the place and it was gone. They didn't make it six months.

They ***could*** have made it. Their desserts were the best, but they just weren't around long enough to build up the customer base that they needed to survive. You have to have longevity—you have to build your base.

You can turn any business, restaurants included, into a success if you work really hard and you manage your cash. It's all about managing cash.

Commandment #2: S-t-r-e-t-c-h Your Marketing Dollars!

"Hotels take reservations. Airlines take reservations. Restaurants take reservations. But only the first two industries are awash in successful loyalty programs. What gives with restaurants?"

–Randolph Hobler, Food Writer

How to Advertise on a Shoestring Budget

Of course, the best way to promote your restaurant or catering service is to provide excellent service and food quality. This will quickly become glowing "word of mouth" advertising for you. But how can you get new patrons to come in and try your place?

Traditional advertising, such as TV or radio ads, can be very expensive for a start-up restaurant. You don't have to spend thousands of dollars on advertising if you spend your money wisely.

Smart marketing is the key.

1. Create a Loyalty Program. Loyalty programs are cheap, easy to implement, and deliver a high return. All they take is a little time and effort. **Loyalty Cards** (buy ten, get one free) are used frequently by coffee shops and cafes. They are good for restaurants too; especially those that offer discounted lunch choices. "Lunch Punch" cards have become a successful way to get repeat business—offer a free lunch after ten visits, and customers will think twice about going somewhere else.

2. Create a menu flyer. Hand it out EVERYWHERE you go. Give it to all the businesses in your local area. Don't be shy! Attach a coupon, or contact the manager or owner of every business near your restaurant and give them a coupon for a free meal. If you deliver great service and get them to come back and recommend their friends, you're already closer to success!

3. Advertise more for special events. If you have the money, spend some real advertising dollars for special events like Father's Day, Secretaries Day, or Mother's Day. These holidays bring big dollars into your restaurant, and you should spend your advertising dollars on the days that bring in the most money.

4. Join your local Chambers of Commerce. Go to their monthly business "mixers." Use the opportunities for networking, cross-promotion, and making new connections. Invite community business owners to patronize your restaurant for free—if they love your food (you know they will!) then they will tell their employees, family, friends, etc. You get the idea. The trick is to get your name out there—once people find out how good your restaurant is, the more they will want to come back!

5. Skip the Yellow Pages and get a website. Yellow Page ads are notoriously expensive, and they generate fewer and fewer referrals every year as the internet takes over as the "go-to" place for information. Maintaining a website is crucial for any business today, and that includes restaurants! If you have some computer skills, you can easily create a nice website using an online template, or you can pay someone to design a nice website for a few hundred dollars. Make sure your menu is online, as well as all your special offerings, such as catering, reservations, or party hosting.

6. Use all the free web resources you can. I am still amazed that some restaurants and clubs don't bother to create a website for themselves, even though it can cost less than $50 per year. In the 21st century, having a website is a necessity.

Your website serves as your online brochure. It works for you twenty-four hours a day, and is always there when a potential customer wants to find information about who you are and what your business has to offer.

Your website will work best for you if it is simple. Your home page should be like a simple company brochure. It should be attractive *and not* about you, but all about the *benefits* that your customers receive by patronizing your restaurant.

Your contact information should be easy to find. Include links to more specific information about your services and credibility. That's it! Keep it simple. If you are in a hurry and don't yet have your own website (which requires your own domain name and a hosting service – inexpensive, but takes a bit of time to set up), all is not lost. There are many social networking sites where, once you join, you are provided a profile page. You can use that as your temporary website if necessary.

I recommend that you create a MySpace page, a Twitter account, and even a free blog on Blogger. None of these networking sites charge you to create a website to promote your business. If you have fifteen minutes, you can create a profile or website through these providers and promote your business online. No matter how busy you are, everyone has at least fifteen minutes to promote their business.

Some "Soft-Sell" Marketing Tricks

Here's a great "soft-sell" tactic that **works**: create an email signature that will list your company name and contact information, as well as any benefit-driven catch phrase that will draw everyone who reads your e-mails to learn more about your business and what you have to offer.

Be sure to include an active link to your website. Every time you send an email, your e-signature is attached, and everyone who gets your email can potentially drive more traffic to your website. It's a very easy way to be sure that everyone you come in contact with via e-mail knows about your business.

"Bounce Back" Marketing for Restaurants

Marketing is maybe the most important function of running a restaurant. It is also the area in which most restaurateurs are the least skilled. That's why I consider lack of marketing skills one of the biggest mistakes restaurants make.

"Bounce back" offers are highly effective for getting repeat business. Collecting customer contact information is the single most important marketing practice a restaurant can undertake.

Don't throw away those business cards! Marketing to customers who have already been to the restaurant gives a better return per marketing dollar than any other practice.

New customers (first timers) represent a huge opportunity for growth for your restaurant. These customers now know what your food is like, what type of value you offer, and where you are located. They have demonstrated that getting to your restaurant is not such a huge hassle that they won't bother coming, and hopefully you've done your job of giving them good food and service at a price they feel comfortable with.

By collecting contact information from these new customers, you have the opportunity to turn them into regular customers. Gaining just one new regular customer per month could mean a $1,000 per year or more sales increase for you, depending on your concept. If it's a couple, or they have children or friends they dine with on a regular basis, it's exponentially more. Since these are all new sales, turning this new customer into a regular customer means growth for you.

Bringing someone back as soon as possible increases your chances of making a permanent impression. They are more likely to remember the server who helped them, how great the food was, and how good a value you offered.

Getting them to bring friends makes them feel more at ease and comfortable. People are more likely to make a restaurant their "hangout" if their friends are there too. By encouraging these new customers to bring guests, you help build the environment necessary to make them comfortable.

Here's a tip: Send out direct mail or e-mail "bounce back" offers to your customers. Give them a reason to come back as soon as possible, with friends. An offer I recommend is to give away a free appetizer, dessert, or specialty beverage to each guest they bring with them. Use the offer as an opportunity to say "thank you," and to entice them back with as many people as you can get them to bring.

Don't offer just any old appetizer or dessert. Offer a particular one so you can use its name or description to make the offer sound more enticing. A "free **Chocolate Avalanche** sundae" sounds a lot better than a "free dessert from our menu." Use this opportunity to promote a signature item. If you don't have signature items, **get some**. People need a good reason to come to you instead of your competition.

A signature item should be something in a particular category, dessert for example, that you make in-house and that is better than the other items in that category. This item should cost more, and contribute more gross profit dollars than your other items, while still being priced low for the incredible quality of the product. This is easily achieved, as your competition probably overcharges for their expensive items because they are worried about "cost percentages" instead of "gross profit dollars." This presents a great opportunity for you to be the best value on the highest quality product. By using this product in your offer, it not only seems like a more impressive offer, but you are also promoting your highest gross profit menu item in that category. You're killing two birds with one stone!

Use this type of a product, and the following verbiage to create an attractive bounce back offer for your new customers:

The reflex of the average restaurateur is to start asking, "How should I limit the offer?", "Should there be a maximum number of desserts I give away?", or "Shouldn't I have a minimum purchase?"

The answer to all those questions is "NO!" The only limitation you should have on a promotional offer is an **expiration date,** because it is there to build urgency and make people "act now" (unless that particular offer is specifically designed to build non-peak time sales).

If you have a good offer that allows you to make money and the customer to experience a good value, then you should want as many people as possible to take advantage of it. The more people your new customers bring with them, the more new customers you can turn into regulars. Even if they bring existing customers with them, they're likely getting those people into your restaurant more than they would have come in on their own. The more friends who come to the restaurant, the more likely they will become regulars.

The only caveat I would throw in would be to warn against using "percent-off" coupons as your promotional offer.

There is nothing unique about a discount. The only thing a discount does is skew your customers' perception of your value. It's easy for them to see what type of value they would have received if they paid the same and didn't receive the free dessert or appetizer, but allowing them to pay less with a percentage or dollar discount gives them bad information to make a value judgment on. This type of promotion also tends to attract "coupon clippers" —people who only go out to eat where they have a coupon. This type of patron isn't likely to come back to your restaurant until the next coupon comes out. You can't build your business on couponing unless you are pricing a 20 percent discount into every menu item, like pizza chains do.

Armed with this marketing tip, I think you'll find not only that your ability to turn new customers into regular customers increases, but also that you'll gain more new customers without having to do the searching yourself. Let your customers be your best salespeople. Offer them something for bringing in their friends. Promote items that make you more money. Get more customers, and make more profit from each of them!

Digital Advertising: Cheaper, Faster, Easier

Unlock the power of the internet! It's cheaper, faster, and easier. Everyone carries a cell phone, but no one carries around a phone book. Put your name on the web and watch your referrals grow.

www.blogger.com: A popular blogging site where you can create a free blog and post photos.

www.meetup.com: This is where you can find targeted local groups to meet with for regular networking events, as well as create a profile page for your business.

www.linkedin.com: A popular social networking site.

www.myspace.com: One of the first social networking sites.

***Important Tip!** When choosing your email address, choose a good email for your business based on your name or business name. Do NOT use a "funny" or "cute" email address. This looks ridiculous to a potential customer and may them disregard your restaurant altogether. It goes without saying that if your email address contains anything "sexual," either overtly or not, it is completely inappropriate. You can get a free email account from Yahoo in just a few minutes.

Don't Throw Away Marketing Information!

No matter how great your product is—if no one knows about it, it won't sell. This fact makes marketing the owner's most important job.

Don't throw away opportunities to communicate with existing customers. In one form or another, customer communication may be the most vital marketing opportunity for a restaurant. Just like your employees, your customers need to know what is going on in your business. So, how do you communicate with them?

Owners have an obligation to build relationships with their customers, and to let them know, with plenty of notice, every special thing that is going to happen in their restaurant. The most effective way to do this is by collecting contact information from existing customers and building a customer database.

A customer database is made up of key facts about every customer who comes into the restaurant. The database should contain customers' first and last names, addresses, and phone and fax numbers whenever possible. E-mail addresses, telephone numbers, and anniversaries can help make contact easier. Special information, such as birthdays, makes it possible to tailor special offers to customers. It may also be helpful to know their favorite dishes, dislikes, and the day the information was collected.

The biggest benefit of a customer database is the ability to spend marketing dollars on customers most likely to come into the restaurant… I'm talking about those who have already been there!

For some owners, spending marketing dollars on people who already know about their business seems like a waste of money, but the truth is that the greatest potential for increasing sales lies with those who already know where you are located, what you sell, and how great a value it is. These are the people who take the least convincing. You already have a relationship with these people.

Think about it —if you were giving away free booze to attract people to a party, who is most likely to come, complete strangers or people who have been to your parties before? Your business is no different. Convincing people to come back more often than they had already planned is much easier that attracting new people, whether it's a house party or a restaurant.

You don't even have to create the database yourself. Pay an employee to come in early and have them enter in the database information into Microsoft Excel or Microsoft Access. Pay them their hourly wage, and offer them a free meal. There are always college students willing to come in to earn a little extra money.

There are several ways to collect customer information. You can simply ask for it by handing out comment cards with blanks to fill in with their information, offer a signup for a "VIP" club, or collect information for a prize giveaway. You may also want to think about contacting other merchants in your area to see if they have customer databases they might like to trade with you. Customers who visit another business close to you are also likely to give you a try since they make regular visits to the area.

Once you collect your customers' information, you have many options on how to use it. With e-mail addresses, you have an almost free way to communicate with your customers. Not all customers have e-mail though, and some who do may not respond to e-mail advertising. Direct mail newsletters are another option to contact customers. Newsletters can be used as more than advertising; you can offer stories about your restaurant, your employees, and your customers.

You may even want to start a "Customer of the Month" contest and publish the winners in your newsletter. Another option is good old fashioned direct mail offers. You can print a postcard with your latest offer or invitation to come to a special event.

***Note:** Direct mail offers sent without a real customer mailing list are a waste of money. Don't purchase mailing lists and send out blind advertising. Save your precious advertising dollars for targeted advertising instead.

Support People Who Support You!

Don't advertise in the yellow pages or use canned mailing lists for useless direct mail advertising. Save your valuable marketing dollars and support those in your community that support you.

When your customers approach you to advertise in the High School yearbook, glee club newsletter, or FFA flyer, then do it. Support loyal customers by making sure that you circulate community dollars back into the community.

If you don't have the money to advertise, offer a gift certificate that they may give away as a prize or a gift. Every little bit helps as a gesture of goodwill.

No matter how you communicate with your customers now, if you don't have a customer database, you're leaving money on the table.

Advertising is crucial to gaining exposure for your restaurant, but you don't have to spend a fortune to drive business to your place. Try to think of creative ways to promote your business without spending money.

"Fishbowls are a big thing. You go in and drop your business card in the fishbowl. Usually the restaurant manager goes in there, gives away the free lunch, and then throws the rest of the cards away."

-**Brian Lambert**, programs manager at Rock Bottom

Interview with the Marketing Expert

Brandon O'Dell
O'Dell Restaurant Consulting
www.bodellconsulting.com
blog.bodellconsulting.com
brandon@bodellconsulting.com
Office: (888) 571-9068

Do you have any specific advice you can give to a new chef or restaurant owner?

Brandon: Marketing is the number one priority, in terms of what a restaurant owner should be doing. It doesn't matter how great your food is—if no one knows about it, it won't sell.

You mention on your website that you think restaurants shouldn't try to appeal to everyone. Explain this concept.

Brandon: One of the biggest mistakes restaurants make is trying to appeal to everyone. I think that restaurant owners need to identify the people that are most likely to patronize their restaurant, and then market ***specifically*** to those people.

There's a very common mistake that restaurant owners make—they will try and be all things to all people. They think that everybody is their target market, so they end up trying to market to everybody. This is incredibly expensive and ineffective, because the amount of marketing dollars that it takes to market to everybody is enormous. It's very important for restaurant owners to narrow in on a specific market. They can use their limited marketing dollars to market ***effectively*** to a smaller market, rather than marketing ***ineffectively*** to a larger market.

What do you feel is the best form of marketing for restaurants? Do you think that radio and print advertising are still viable marketing tools?

Brandon: Well, radio and print advertising are good when you have a specific event to market. For brand building, however, it's often too expensive for the average restaurant. It's not a large enough return on the dollar, but for specific events, such as a Grand Opening, or to advertise a particular special, it can be effective. But otherwise it's a waste of money.

I have found that the most effective marketing method is developing a customer database and marketing to existing customers. Whether it's through direct mail or email, marketing to your existing customers returns far more on the dollar than any other form of advertising. Email marketing is especially great because it's so cheap.

There's different software available that can help owners track their customers and market to them directly. **Fishbowl** and **Constant Contact** are two companies that offer software solutions to marketing to existing customers. They are primarily email based, but they can be used for direct mail marketing as well.

Collecting existing customer contact information and using that information should be the "heart and soul" of a restaurant's marketing program.

How do you recommend that owners collect their existing customer information? Some customers don't like sharing that information.

Brandon: One of the most popular ways is to create a "VIP" or "customer loyalty" program. You basically offer some sort of reward for customers to offer their contact information, such as free meals on birthdays or anniversaries, or "member only" discount days you can use to build sales during slow periods.

The customer doesn't see it as a marketing ploy to which they would have a natural resistance. The customer sees the program as a benefit for them.

So you don't advocate standard direct mail marketing?

The last report that I read said that standard direct mail marketing, which targets people who *haven't* been to your restaurant, had an average return rate of about one-half of one percent. That's a terrible return. But restaurant owners that use direct mail marketing using an existing customer database have seen a return rate as high as 40-50 percent. The difference in customer response is staggering.

That's a huge difference.

Brandon: We've seen similar returns on email marketing when it's used for a "Birthday Club" or "Anniversary Club" to existing customers. It's just a standard email, with a simple offer to the individual customer. The response rate can be as high as 50 percent for birthday and anniversary club offers just as with direct mail to existing customers, but even average response rates of 15-20 percent are common when offers are properly structured.

The difference in response and return on investment is much higher if the loyalty program offers are structured correctly.

Well, when a restaurant is having problems, what do you recommend to the owners? Do you generally suggest a marketing solution?

Brandon: Marketing is what restaurant owners have the least knowledge of, so they tend to need the most help from me in that area. But you can't have a strong marketing campaign until you have your pricing structure set up correctly.

While I believe that marketing is the single most important thing, it won't be successful unless a restaurant addresses two other key issues first:

1. There have to be good control systems in place to reduce employee theft, limit waste, and reduce liability, including a proper inventory system.

2. The restaurant must have their products priced properly.

One thing that very few chefs do, but I always stress the importance of, is the practice of comparing their actual physical inventory with an "**ideal inventory.**" Their physical inventory should be used to create a Cost of Goods Sold (COGS). I stress that chefs should compare their actual COGS to their **"ideal"** COGS. This is figured by taking their current recipe costs and multiplying those costs by their sales by item.

Chefs can use this technique to figure out what their food SHOULD have cost them to sell, compared to what it actually cost to sell. If there is a significant difference between those two numbers, this points to either waste or theft.

Theft and waste are big issues for chefs and restaurant owners. It seems to be a common problem in the hospitality industry.

Brandon: Normally, what I've seen in failing restaurants—the theft problem is directly connected to poor management controls. There's a direct relationship there. The weaker the management controls, the more likely the theft. It's like nobody's watching the henhouse. It really has less to do with the quality of employees, as it does with the quality of management systems.

Do you feel that employees will be more apt to steal if they feel like their management isn't watching?

Brandon: Yes, if there's more opportunity, there will be more theft. And this holds true for waste as well. Poor portioning, bad inventory controls, etc. They all have their root cause in poor management. Owners have to keep their "eyes on the prize," so to speak.

One of the other big cost issues for restaurants is the reduction of employee accidents. What do you feel that chefs can do to reduce accidents in the kitchen specifically, because this seems to be the area where accidents happen most often?

Brandon: I think training is more important than anything. Industrial and manufacturing businesses always use a written safety manual. In a restaurant, you rarely ever see a safety manual except in the bigger corporate restaurants.

Smaller restaurants rarely have written procedures, and employees are more likely to injure themselves if written procedures aren't in place.

Other than the marketing issue, the other most important factor I see contributing to the failure of restaurants is their pricing procedures.

You mean problems with menu pricing?

Brandon: Normally, restaurants choose a target food cost percentage and use that as the basis for their menu pricing. They completely ignore the other costs associated with running a restaurant. One thing I'll never forgive formal culinary schools and corporate chain restaurants for is teaching new, impressionable would-be chefs to use a budgeted cost percentage to price food menus. These chefs become owners who are so fixated on a target food cost, say 30 percent, that they create prices for menu items based solely on that 30 percent, basically ignoring the other 70 percent of the costs of running a restaurant.

Food costs make up anywhere from 20-40 percent of the financial picture in most restaurants. Depending on labor costs, food cost could be the largest expense of running a restaurant business, and it needs consideration when forming menu prices. BUT… What about the other 60-80 percent of the financial picture? It's not all profit.

This is a radical concept— there are a lot of people that will disagree with you on this one!

Brandon: Absolutely. I blame culinary schools and chain restaurants for hammering the idea that cost percentage is the best way to price out a menu. Chain restaurants share an equal responsibility for perpetuating this bad practice by focusing their managers on food cost percentages without letting them in on the secret that the cost percentage is a *management tool*, not a *pricing tool.*

I guess the question is how can chefs price by gross profit?

Brandon: Unlike the menu price, the needed gross profit per person is a fluid number. You can't throw prices out there, whether based on cost percentages or gross profit, without considering what your market is already paying for those products elsewhere. Just like your potential customers, you must consider what other operations are charging for the same type of food, or even the same dishes, that you are offering.

I tell chefs to focus on developing a *"target gross profit dollar,"* per customer, rather than a food cost percentage per menu item. Owners need to figure out how much it costs to serve every person that walks through their door. They can do it pretty easily by using their profit and loss statement and their customer count numbers.

All they have to do is take all their business costs, (the cost of running their restaurant) and the projected profit target, and subtract out the cost of food. Then, take that number and divide it by the number of customers that walk through their doors, and the resulting number will give you the needed gross profit per customer—that is essentially the markup that they need to make from each customer in order to pay their costs. Once they add the needed markup to the actual cost of the menu item, they get a price that not only pays for the cost of the food, but also the cost of all the expenses of running the restaurant, in addition to the profit they need to make.

They can use an average of all months' expenses by using a year-end profit and loss statement. From the P&L, chefs need to find how much all their operating expenses are for the year without including product costs. This is the overhead cost. To this, add the ideal profit the restaurant ***should have made*** (the "ideal profit") during that time period.

Formula:
Total expenses for year - product costs + ideal profit = Total needed gross profit

This is a better guideline to create menu prices that deliver that much needed gross profit to pay those expenses. It's a little more complicated than that, because there are a lot of variables that go into the actual equation such as a particular market's price point and what their competitors are charging, but that's one of the things I teach restaurant owners how to do. I teach them how to figure out how to price out their menu in order to deliver a target gross profit for each customer that walks through their door, while still offering a great value. More often than not, owners find they can actually charge *less* for many of their menu items and still make more profit.

As long as the chef keeps their recipe costs up to date, they will get the profit that they price for as long as they maintain or grow their existing customer base.

It sounds like you are a big advocate of this method. Does it work?

Brandon: Well, mathematically speaking, there's no way for it NOT to work. Restaurants need a certain amount of mark-up to make money. If you have a certain number of people walking through your door, and you are controlling your expenses at least to the point as you were when you created your prices, then you will make the profit you calculated into the process. Of course, the restaurant will still have to have at least the same number of customers as when you created the analysis. At that point, it becomes a matter of creating control systems to make sure that your expenses are where they should be, and a marketing plan that keeps customers coming through your door.

We're back to the marketing issue.

Brandon: Yes. After we establish a needed gross profit and prices to achieve the target profit, and the management is concentrating on marketing, we're then prepared to see the profit grow by leaps and bounds.

Any other suggestions?

Brandon: Well, another concept that I think is important is the "unique selling point." This is also called a "unique selling proposition." To me, the core of a marketing plan is having something unique that the business chooses to market directly to their customers as their primary product. I help the restaurant owner choose an EMOTION to sell to their customers, and treat this emotion above their food or their service.

Reason being, claims about great food and service are **not unique**. Every restaurant claims to have great food and service. While it is incredibly important to have good food and service, by doing so the restaurant owner is only *meeting* the expectations of the patron. They need something beyond food and service to *exceed* them.

Explain that— what you mean by "selling an emotion?"

Brandon: Well, a good example is Hard Rock Cafe. They sell [rock] nostalgia. They're creating a connection with people that love rock memorabilia. In their business, the food is really secondary. I bet you can't tell me any item that's on the Hard Rock Cafe menu, but you have an expectation of what the restaurant is about, just based on their name. You go inside, and you might see Michael Jackson's glove, or Elvis's jumpsuit. Customers don't go there for the food. They go there to see the rock memorabilia. They are selling a concept.

Another example is the Hooters chain. Their food is secondary, in my opinion. The wings are pretty good, but the rest of the food is marginal. Their main product is sex—it isn't food. They dress girls in shorts and tight tops and, as a result, it's mostly men that patronize the chain. The male customers enjoy being flirted with. Hooters has recognized that there is a demand for sex, and the food is secondary.

So, you are saying that the restaurant concept is should be primary.

Brandon: Yes, the food should be great, and back up the unique selling point, but the entire restaurant concept—the name, the location, the menu items—everything should be designed around that unique selling point. The restaurant owner needs to decide who is underserved in the market, and find the unique selling point that is going to work in that market.

A unique selling point still has to match your own strengths. Your unique selling point still has to mesh with the type of restaurant that you want to run, and are capable of running.

For example, I had a customer that owned a middle-priced bistro. He had great food and a menu that changed every single week. He already had a good customer following, so when we were trying to find a unique selling point for him, a natural fit was "excitement and change." Since the owner was already doing things to reinforce the concept, all the owner had to do was embrace that unique selling point. Then, every time he does a mailer or a print ad, he can reinforce that unique selling point to further brand his restaurant.

A caveat to all the focus on marketing and price, and one thing I don't want to confuse restaurant owners on is the importance of having food that meets or exceeds the expectations of your customers.

While McDonalds may be able to please their customers with small, frozen hamburger patties, that doesn't mean that every restaurant can as long as they have a strong concept. Every restaurant's food must meet or exceed the expectations of their customers if they want to stay in business. If their expectations are low, the food must still be as good as their low expectations. If a restaurant has led patrons to believe they have incredible food, then they darn well better.

Ultimately, the patron's choice of whether or not to eat at a restaurant again will come down to **value**. Did they get their money's worth? If the answer is "no," then no amount of marketing, control systems, or pricing philosophy is going to keep the doors open.

Commandment #3: Create a More Profitable Menu

"Large menus have a lot of downfalls. They require excessive prep, cause long ticket times, are hard to educate service staff on and generally drive down profitability. Keep your menu focused on your concept, and easy to produce."

-Brandon O'Dell, O'Dell Restaurant Consulting

Create a Menu Concept that Can Succeed

One of the most important aspects of running a lucrative kitchen is designing a profitable menu. Your menu should match the restaurant's concept, and you should closely monitor how well each individual dish performs.

Ultimately, you have to be flexible in order to have a profitable menu. According to Restaurants USA magazine, a well-designed menu can improve overall sales from 2-10 percent.

Labor and food costs are always high in any restaurant, so a smart menu needs to have a good balance of high-profit items to balance out the more expensive steak and seafood items. All high-cost menu items should be matched with an item with a low food cost percentage. Make sure that you know the dollar amounts as well as the profit percentages of each dish. It's always easier to raise the price on a few dishes rather than cut labor. Most professional restaurant consultants agree that most restaurants can sneak a few price increases into their menus without their customers noticing. Design your profit right **into the menu**.

Have a policy to remove poorly-performing menu items. Try to remove your weakest items (maybe as often as once a week). Use the space to introduce a new item with good money-making potential. Think about your specials. Do you have a stellar performer? Consider making it a regular menu item. You can also consider rotating dishes based on the season. Fresh salads, chilled fruits, and blended drinks will sell better in the Summertime. Comfort foods, hot drinks, and soups will sell better in the Winter.

Ditch side dishes that people won't eat. Ask your dishwasher and your servers about the side dishes. Which side dishes are getting thrown away or not eaten? Remove these poor performers.

Always make sure you have a nice offering of drinks, side orders, and desserts on your menu. All these items make money and boost profits. Hot drinks, such as specialty coffees, hot chocolate and tea pots do well when the weather gets cold. Non alcoholic blended drinks, such as milkshakes and fruity power shakes do well when it's hot. The profit margin on specialty drinks is enormous. It's a great way to increase per-customer ticket averages, too. Try adding a table tent with all your specialty drinks and desserts to each dining table.

Make sure you always have a good offering of coffee, iced tea, hot tea, hot chocolate, and lemonade. These are all high-profit items. It's easy to make money when you sell a product that's mostly water. Since most restaurants charge about $2 for drinks, avoid giving tap water to your guests unless they specifically ask for it, since this almost always leads to reduced sales.

When you design your menu, don't preoccupy yourself so much with the actual profit percentage. A lot of chefs obsess about the percentage of food cost for a particular item, but the actual net dollars contributed by an item is just as important.

Actual profit can even be more important, especially when a restaurant is starting up and cash flow is tight. You still need to make payroll! For example, a $1.50 cup of tea that costs just .05 cents to make has a whopping profit of 97 percent, but the actual dollar amount of profit is still only $1.45. On the other hand, a T-Bone steak dinner that sells for $19 and costs $7 to make has a profit of only 63 percent, but an actual return of $12. More money in the register is always good. Those extra dollars really add up!

There are many tips that can help boost food sales just by having a good menu design.

Top Ten Menu Design Mistakes

1. Price Validation: Move your prices into the description of the items. This way, it makes it harder for your customers to "fish" for the cheapest item on your menu. Make them focus on the descriptions of the product, rather than the price. It helps to remove the dollar sign from the price, as well.

2. Use Boxing: Add variety to your menu design by using "boxing." Your bestsellers and high-profit seafood items should be "boxed" to make them stand out. This can boost sales of a particular item by 10-15 percent.

2. Item Placement: People's eyes naturally go to the right-hand corner of the menu first, and customers tend to remember the last two items and the first two. Place your high-profit items at the top and bottom of your menu, and place the cheaper items dispersed in the center.

4. Page Positioning on a Three-Panel Menu: If you use a three-panel menu, people will look at the center panel first and then at the other two panels. Try boxing your signature item right in the middle of the center panel with a nice description. You can also use this position for high-profit specials or signature drinks.

5. Keep it Short but Sweet: It's best to keep your descriptions of the dishes short. Customers want a nice description, but don't go overboard. When possible, use photographs. A cluttered menu is hard on the eyes and drives some customers crazy.

6. Highlight Certain Food Types: If you have a large menu selection, it's a good idea to place like items together. Instead of an "Entrees" page, try putting "Fresh Salads," "Seafood Dishes," or "Our Specialties" in their own spot. This allows your customers to find a certain type of dish faster. Use color icons to let your customer know about a menu item—whether it's spicy, healthy, etc.

7. Don't Use a Tiny Font: It goes without saying that you should make your menus easy to read. If your customers are over fifty, then menus with a tiny typeface are going to be annoying. If you see your customers holding the menus out at arm's length, or bringing them up to squint, then consider going to a larger font.

8. Include a Side-Dish Section: Make sure your menu has a selection of side dishes and add-ons. These tend to be very profitable for restaurants, and it helps increase your check average with no effort. You can also create unique side dishes that sound expensive but are really profit-makers for your restaurant.

9. Don't Skip Dessert: Offer a nice selection of desserts and dessert coffees. Keep a table tent on the table so customers can flip through the dessert selections and whet their appetite. Desserts can easily boost check averages, and take little or no time to prepare.

10. Keep your menus clean: Customers will always associate a dirty menu with a dirty restaurant. Use protective covers and throw menus away when they are tattered or dirty. First impressions matter! Make sure the hostess has window cleaner and a towel to wipe off dirty menus. Invest in laminated menus because they are the easiest to clean. Tell servers to be careful when giving a menu to a guest. Menus should all be cleaned at the end of the night as part of the hostess's side work.[6]

Keep it Simple

I'm going to talk about a key fundamental in restaurant concept design called "***keeping it simple.***" There is a silent killer in restaurants—a bloated menu. These are big menus with too many items, multi-ingredient dishes, huge liquor selections, and wine lists. They're all symptoms of the same problem: overcomplicating your concept.

As a restaurateur, you may find yourself getting bored with traditional menu items. For you, eating in a restaurant might need to be an adventure. You may have to see or try something you've never seen before to be impressed.

This may be the underlying factor in why chefs routinely go overboard when designing their menu concepts. Chefs push their own sensibilities on the general public, not realizing that their tastes are not indicative of the tastes of the public at large. Restaurateurs think that carrying fifteen bourbons instead of five will earn them more customers. If you have a larger selection, you'll appeal to more people, right? **Wrong.**

---

[6] Softcafe Menu Marketing Tips, used with permission. www.softcafe.com/menu-marketing.htm

Trying to please everyone leaves your concept undefined. You'll find it harder to manage your business effectively and market your brand. Cut out all the extras and keep it simple.

Here's a short list of things you can do to keep your concept simple.

1. Keep your menu selection small. This serves many purposes. A small menu is easier to control costs on, easier to prepare and order for, and easier to provide consistency with. By having a small menu, your service will be faster, your food quality will be better, and you'll make more money. Keep your menu simple.

2. Choose two contrasting but complementary colors to design your concept. You may use a third neutral color for accenting, but stay away from unneeded detail and too many extra colors in your scheme. To create a solid brand, you need to be memorable, and that means keeping your color scheme simple. Use these colors to design your logo, signage, marketing, and to decorate the inside and outside of your restaurant.

3. Keep your dining room simple. Smaller dining rooms are easier to manage. A large dining room takes a large management staff and lots of employees to run.

4. Keep your target market simple. Don't convince yourself that you want all people of all demographics to like your business. It's not going to happen. By going after "everyone," you'll end up with no one. Even if your style of cooking has mass appeal, your location will determine who is most likely to come into your restaurant.

Are you located by a Catholic Church, a local park, or a shopping center? That is your target market (whether you like it or not). Identify the person's age, income level, sex, marital status, and religion. If your concept doesn't appeal to the people in your local area, then you aren't likely to succeed. Keep your demographic focused.

5. Keep your actual menu dishes simple. When you have too many ingredients, and/or too many touches that need to be made to the dish after it's ordered and before it goes out, you slow down the production of your food. A completed ticket will only go out as fast as its slowest dish. Keep your food simple and easy to produce. Let the ingredients be the stars and don't lose them in a mish-mash of garnishes.

6. Don't try to carry every liquor. If you don't carry Glenfiddich, but you do have five other single malt scotches, reasonable customers are not going to overlook your restaurant next time because you don't carry their particular brand. It is more important for you to have a manageable inventory and a selection small enough for your staff to become knowledgeable on than it is to try to please every customer's sense of taste.

I've got a secret for you. Even if you carry fifty different vodkas, you'll still end up with someone requesting one you don't have. Keep your liquor and wine selection simple.

Any time you have the opportunity to simplify your concept, take it. You'll end up with something that is simpler to manage, simpler to market, and simpler to turn a profit with.

Maximize Profits with Best Menu Practices

1. Always use a printed menu insert for your specials. This one may seem obvious but many restaurateurs don't realize that specials should be printed rather than recited. It is a rare individual who can verbally outsell a printed menu. Offering an 'up-sell' suggestion about a particular special is not a bad idea, but reciting the entire list is. The specials should appear on a menu insert or menu page that is separate from your regular menu to further distinguish them and to facilitate daily or weekly changes. Direct your servers to point out the daily specials, and have them mention the up-sells, such as "sautéed mushrooms for just 3.99."

2. "Above 5, add 95": Since pricing increments of less than $1 don't change the value of perception for an item that it is priced at more than $5, add $.95 on any special that's more than $5. For example, since $13.50 and $13.95 have the same perceived value, go with $13.95 to maximize your profits.

3. Offer experimental dishes as a daily special: Offer each new item as a special. It's a great way to test a new dish. If the special sells consistently, or customers start asking for it on days that it isn't offered, consider moving it onto the main menu. If the new dish is a bust, you don't have to worry since you can drop it without affecting your regular menu.

4. Keep them coming back with variety: Your best and most frequent customers will eventually tire of the same menu over and over. A variety of specials will keep things fresh and keep them coming back. You can also post specials on your website, allowing your customers to check in and see if their favorite dish is being served.

5. Use dessert and beverage table tents: If you operate a restaurant where table tents are appropriate, consider using them for dessert and beverage specials. Table tents used in this fashion can double sales from these two highly profitable categories since they continue to "sell" after the regular menus have been taken away. [7]

6. Use a fancy typeface: Really! People perceive complicated fonts to mean complex foods that need greater skill to prepare, according to a University of Michigan study. So, customers **perceive** that dishes are "fancier" if they are described in a fancy typeface. See below:

Herb-crusted baked cod, brown rice pilaf, fresh green beans, steamed $14.50

See the difference?

Herb-crusted baked cod, brown rice pilaf, fresh green beans, steamed $14.50

If you own your own restaurant, use professional design software to design your menus. The menus will look more professional, and the design will be easier to change frequently, even daily, if you decide to offer daily specials. The best software on the market for menu design is MenuPro, by Softcafé. It costs less than the Microsoft Suite, and it is worth the money. Over 10,000 restaurants use Softcafé software,

[7] Maximize your Profits with Specials, Softcafé, used with permission.

and they have a money-back guarantee, which is rare for software providers. The software is easy to use, not full of bugs, and good for restaurants, bars, etc.

If you cannot afford professional menu software, use a nice template on Microsoft Word or other word processing software, but use fine paper at least. One of the worst things you can do is appear "cheap" or unprofessional. Professionally designed menus look sharp and they are the first impression that your customer sees when they sit down.

Softcafé also has a complete software suite for restaurant owners (which include employee scheduling software and restaurant website software). You can get information on the software on their website: ***www.softcafe.com***.[8] (The authors have no financial interest in and receive no compensation from manufacturers of products or websites mentioned in this book.)

7. Consider taking your menu online: Have you thought about allowing customers to order online? Now with the internet on every cell phone, you can make it easier and more convenient for your business clients to order a quick lunch on the go. How about a catering order for a big meeting? Make sure that you have a nice, straightforward website that details your menu, contact information, and basic information about your restaurant. Stay away from adding music or animation—it's slower to load and some people may just get frustrated by it.

---

[8] MenuPro, ScheduleWriter, WebGuider, and SoftCafe are registered trademarks of SoftCafe, LLC. MenuPro protected by U.S. Patent No. D451,101, and D474,196.
Other Patents Pending. MenuPro is a registered trademark of SoftCafe, LLC

Commandment #4: Eliminate Employee Accidents!

"The average foodservice facility will experience up to ten incidents per year with an average claim amount ranging from $1,000 - $3,000, not including lost time."

-Steve Hall, Director of Operations, Ecolab

Zero-Tolerance Policies Work!

Employee accidents cause bad publicity, lower employee morale, and increase insurance costs. The National Safety Council reports that the average cost per disabling injury in the United States is $28,000, including lost wages, medical expenses, administrative expenses, and employer costs.

The government estimates that up to ***nine million*** accidents per year are attributable to slips and falls. This accident is the most common of almost 500,000 accidents occurring nationwide to restaurant employees. The annual cost to businesses is $3.5 billion, according to the U.S. Bureau of Labor Statistics.

Falls are the most common accident in foodservice. Back injuries and other fall-related accidents cost restaurant owners millions of dollars every year, and in every case, prevention is always cheaper than trying to heal the employee later. All restaurants must have a strict uniform and shoe policy. Chefs also **MUST** insist that all their cooks and other employees wear shoes with slip-resistant soles. If you have not instituted a policy like this beforehand, just be firm and institute the policy immediately. The employees will get used to the idea, and in a few months they will not even think twice about it.

Eliminate Employee Drinking

Do not allow employees to consume alcohol in your restaurant, even if they are off the clock. What if that employee gets into an auto accident later on that evening? Even if they went drinking somewhere else, there's proof that they drank at your restaurant. How much legal liability will you have in this situation? The only answer is to eliminate employee drinking all together. Let staff know the real cost of your liability and worker's comp insurance. It may raise some eyebrows and will help send the point home.

Even if you allowed the practice in the past, tell your employees that your insurance company has increased your premiums and now you must discontinue the practice. If employees want to drink after their shifts, there are other restaurants where they can go. Heavy drinkers can find another place to work. They are a liability anyway.

If a staff member (especially a cook, who has a higher risk of cutting injuries) comes to work and complains that he was out "partying all night," seriously consider sending him home. Exhausted and hung-over employees are a huge safety liability.

Use Cutting Gloves Every Time!

In my kitchen, employees are immediately reprimanded in writing if they neglect to use cutting gloves. After three warnings, the employee is fired. You must institute a **zero-tolerance policy** for the use of cutting gloves. Although no glove (even steel mesh) will prevent all cuts, they greatly reduce the chance of cutting accidents.

Each cutting accident can cost a restaurant thousands of dollars in increased insurance costs, worker's compensation, and accident and disability claims.

Employees who work on a meat cutting saw or process poultry or beef should always use a metal mesh glove. Employees should also use a metal glove when sharpening knives. Because the metal conducts heat, it is generally better for employees to use a cloth or Kevlar glove while they are cooking, in order to prevent burns.

The use of cutting gloves is equally important in the dish area, where dishwashers regularly handle knives, cutting equipment, and broken glass.

Some gloves have drawbacks. For example, a metal glove is made of fine stainless steel mesh. Although the metal gloves give superior cut and puncture protection, they may trap bacteria and must be cleaned using bleach or other highly sanitizing methods. We use a commercial-strength sanitizer to sanitize all of our mesh gloves. Mesh gloves are resistant to water, chemicals, and offer the best cut protection.

Chefs should also order a large amount of cotton cutting gloves for your kitchen staff to use when they are doing all other low-risk tasks.

Cotton gloves provide minimal cut resistance, but they are inexpensive, easy to clean, and a great alternative for new chefs trying to save money. Cotton gloves still reduce accidents. It is still much more difficult to cut through a cotton cutting glove vs. a bare hand.

Make sure that you purchase cutting gloves to fit all your staff— female cooks will most likely need small gloves, while male cooks will use medium to large. Other pointers to reduce cutting accidents:

1. Always store knives neatly on a magnetic strip or a butcher's block. Never store knives loose in a drawer.
2. Knives should always be washed by hand, not by machine, and dishwashers should use cutting gloves at all times in order to prevent cutting accidents from knives and broken glass.
3. Have knives sharpened regularly. Do not allow cooks to use dull knives. This forces the cooks to use more pressure to cut food products, which increases cutting accidents.
4. A rusty or dirty knife should never come in contact with food. Either throw old knives away, or send them to be oiled and sharpened. A professional sharpening service can save you money in the long run.
5. Do not allow cooks to leave knives unattended. Knives should always be in use or put away safely. Do regular "kitchen safety sweeps" to make sure that knives are put away properly.

Require the Use of Non-Skid Shoes

We enforce a mandatory uniform policy: a black shirt, a black or white chef coat, chef's pants, black socks, and slip-resistant shoes.

If the employee comes to work without the correct uniform, he or she is offered the opportunity to correct the infraction by purchasing the missing article of clothing. In our restaurants, if an employee does not wear slip-resistant shoes, he or she will be sent home and not allowed to work the shift.

The most well-known website to purchase slip-resistant shoes is ***www.shoesforcrews.com***. **SHOES FOR CREWS®** are the highest rated in the industry against slips and falls. You may want to offer the shoes to your new employees in the form of a salary advance. This will help defray the costs for the employee, and it also ensures that your employees will start their shift wearing the footwear that you require in order to prevent accidents.

SHOES FOR CREWS® also provides slip-resistant floor mats at affordable prices.

Help Reduce Employee Burns

Chefs and kitchen managers all know that kitchen fires are a reality and employees are always at risk for burns. Chefs should always have a written fire policy. You should be unwavering in its application. Reprimand employees who do not follow the policy.

Hot oil burns are a considerable hazard for workers who use deep fat fryers. Workers can be badly burned if the oil or grease is not allowed to cool before handling.

Chemical burns can result from unsafe handling of cleaning supplies, especially highly acidic or alkaline cleaning solvents. Cleaning supplies and disinfectants can cause serious injuries if they come in contact with skin or eyes. Make sure eye wash is always available.

> A sixteen-year-old girl was employed at a fast-food outlet to cook fries at a frying range. She slipped on water leaking from an ice-making machine and instinctively put out her hand to break her fall. Unfortunately her hand went into the deep fat fryer containing oil at a temperature of 360°F and she sustained severe burns to her left hand and forearm.
>
> *-Euro Agency for Safety and Health at Work*

Easy Safety Tips

The simplest safety tips are common sense solutions to accident prevention. You have a moral and legal duty to make sure your employees and customers are safe from accidents and contaminated foods.

1. Employees should wear appropriate clothing while around open-flame appliances or hot surfaces; loose-fitting long sleeved shirts or open jackets should not be allowed near any cooking surface. Polyester clothing attracts heat, so encourage your cooks to purchase cotton clothing for its breathability and comfort.
2. All long hair should be up and confined, not only for sanitary reasons, but for safety reasons. Prohibit the use of hair spray, which is flammable.
3. Prohibit the use of all jewelry (rings can cause severe burns on the fingers, and necklaces can get caught in machinery).
4. Unplug portable appliances when they are not in use, and keep all cords away from hot surfaces, water, and sinks! If a wire burns out, it can cause a very serious electrical burn.
5. Keep hot surfaces free from combustibles: Cotton potholders, boxes, plastic utensils, etc. should all be kept away from hot surfaces. Require the use of gloves for any employee working the grill or the oven.
6. Always keep a first aid kit stocked, with burn spray, antiseptic wipes, eye wash, bandages, and other first aid must-haves. Sometimes early intervention and a quick response will save a trip to the doctor!

Just one trip to the emergency room can erase months of savings from all your other cost-saving techniques. Plus, no one wants to see a valuable employee go home or to the hospital because of an accident!

Karen's Story

I've owned a small breakfast and lunch casual-dining restaurant for about twelve years. The cost of our liability insurance was killing us! I finally got fed up and instituted a no-tolerance policy requiring all employees (including servers and hostesses) to purchase slip-resistant shoes. Any employee that did not comply got sent home. A few complained, but eventually everyone complied. There have been ***no falls*** since we instituted the policy, and we also instituted a policy for the use of mandatory cutting gloves (which we provide to all the cooks).

Our insurance costs have been cut by half, and they continue to decrease. We now have a safety reward program, and the employees all get their names put in a raffle for a $100 gas card every month that we don't have an accident. It's been great! I just wish I'd done it sooner. [9]

Create a Safety Culture

Create a safety culture in your kitchen. Employee safety incentive programs have great results. Do a quick audit of the workplace safety in your restaurant and find out if you have work to do!

1. You consistently talk about workplace safety.
2. You have written penalties for safety infractions, and they are enforced consistently.

[9] Names have been changed.

3. You have trained your employees on the difference between safe and unsafe behavior, and the penalties that result from unsafe behavior (written warning, firing, reprimand, etc).
4. You reward employees who practice and promote exemplary safe behavior.
5. Employees are required to use slip-resistant shoes, cutting gloves, and protective hairnets to prevent food contamination.
6. You hold regular safety meetings that all employees are required to attend.

Safety Training is the Key

Make sure all of your employees are well-trained in your safety program. Don't cut corners, and have a written policy in place. Make sure every employee understands the safety policy, and signs it. Be firm when safety rules are broken.

So don't skimp on safety—every dollar you spend on safety measures saves you three to five dollars over time, so it's money well spent!

Commandment #5: Stop Employee Theft

"The typical independent restaurant loses approximately 4 to 5 percent of sales to theft every single year."

-The National Restaurant Association

Don't Ignore Red Flags!

Small businesses, especially restaurants, are prime targets for employee theft. The U.S. Chamber of Commerce estimates that most employee theft goes undetected, and the possibility of theft increases when economic times are bad. The National Restaurant Association estimates that internal employee theft is responsible for 75 percent of inventory shortages. This is a staggering **4 percent** of total restaurant sales!

Employee theft costs businesses $40 billion each year. This amount is TEN TIMES the losses from street crime in the United States. The government reports that up to one-third of employees steal at some point in their careers. Employee theft includes:

1. Faking an injury for compensation
2. Taking food, liquor, or other merchandise
3. Putting fictitious employees on the payroll
4. Stealing cash from the registers (skimming)
5. Using fake coupons, gift cards, etc. (common in restaurants)

Employee theft usually occurs because of a breakdown in procedure. As an owner, manager or chef, you are ultimately responsible for the employees under your direction.

Establish a written policy about employee theft, and do not apply a double-standard to some employees, and not to others.

Avoid double-standards. Establish a clear policy in writing. Always be thoughtful of other employee's reactions and possible repercussions. Take the employee aside and offer them the chance to explain. Did they pay for the item out of pocket? Did they ask permission from another manager? Deal with each employee on a case-by-case basis, but still try to stick to the policies that you have in place.

The "Good Employee" Dilemma

Sandra, your best server, always arrives early and helps to set up the restaurant. She sweeps, cleans, sets the tables, and does everything efficiently. She makes herself a milkshake and eats it in the back while she is waiting for tables. You don't quibble because Sandra comes in early every single day and works without complaint. She always covers shifts when you call, as well.

Daniel, another server, is always trying to sneak in late. He tries to avoid doing his side work, never sweeps, or helps clean the back area. He already has two write-ups for tardiness. Daniel comes in this morning, sees Sandra making a milkshake, and decides to make one for himself, too.

As the chef, this infuriates you, because you think Daniel is lazy and doesn't deserve it. You give Daniel a write-up for stealing food (the milkshake). Daniel responds that it is "discrimination" because Sandra was eating a milkshake too, and you didn't say anything to her.

See the dilemma?

Owners often choose to ignore warning signs because they want to believe their employees are honest. But the truth of the matter is that employees who steal will continue to do so until they get caught. Here are ten tips:

1. **Have your food costs or liquor costs gone up suddenly?** This is one of the prime examples of when a good inventory will save you! If food costs suddenly go up, this may point to a new manager or cook. If liquor costs go up, a new bartender may be stealing. If costs go DOWN dramatically, look for who is on vacation, on maternity leave, or away from the restaurant. You may have caught your thief with good inventory practices!
2. **Track employee sales, and do regular audits.** Make sure that you track every employee's sales, and do regular audits of servers' cash and bar tills. For the kitchen staff, make sure that a manager is present when the staff goes out to throw away the trash for the evening, both for the employee's safety and also to prevent theft. Lock up all premium items, such as premium liquor, lobsters, steaks, and shrimp.
3. **Create a tracking sheet to count high-cost items.** Always track high-cost items, such as lobster, prime meats, and expensive shellfish when it comes into the restaurant. A full count of these items should be made at the end of the night and checked against sales. Comps and sales should be equal to the number of items missing from the tracking sheet. Any irregularities should cause a red flag.
4. **Invest in a meat cage.** A good meat cage is worth every penny. A meat cage usually costs between $250-$400. But remember that it is only good if you remember to lock it!
5. **Do trash audits.** Employees are creative when they steal. Most cooks who steal take the product out in a garbage can and then take it to their car later. Trash audits can also discover lots of inadvertent waste

too—like dozens of forks, spoons, and ramekins thrown in the trash by frenzied servers and dishwashers.

6. **Invest in a good security camera system.** This is well worth the price. Make the cameras obvious to the employees, and place them in the bar and on the cooks' line, and anywhere else that you feel employees may steal, such as in the hallway by the walk-in freezer.
7. **Maintain your back door locked and alarmed.** Your back door should always be locked and alarmed, and should be rigged as a fire exit. **Detex Alarms** are some of the best in the business, and I prefer their alarms, although there are a number of good alarm companies to choose from. Detex Manufactures security door hardware, exit alarms, control locks, electronic access control, and accessories. Their website is ***www.detex.com.***
8. **Limit access to the safe and cash**. Only the managers, owners, or the chef should have access to the safe and the registers. Make sure the safe combination is changed regularly, at least once a week. Do regular register drops during a busy shift. This protects the bartender and your business in case of a hold-up.
9. **Watch employees' personal behavior**. Watch for warning signs. Trust your gut. Is an employee acting out of character, or overly-diligent in the job? Look for warning signs of substance abuse—they need extra money to finance the habit. Watch for a bad attitude, or complaining about management to other employees. Also, if you discover that the employee was terminated for theft by a former employer, look out!

10. **Make yourself visible at all times**. The best defense against employee theft is to make sure you are personally involved in running the restaurant. The more visible you are, the less of a chance an employee has to steal. Ask questions, and rotate through the restaurant as much as possible so your presence is felt.

The Rib Thief

Manuel was a cook putting full racks of ribs in plastic bags and throwing them away with the trash, only to go out later "for a cigarette," take the ribs out of the trash, and take them home. Before he was caught, the losses in meat every night were huge. We knew that someone was stealing, but it still took at least another two weeks of diligent detective work and trash audits to find the culprit.

Give Incentives NOT to Steal

Never assume that long-time or trusted employees will resist the temptation to steal. Drug addiction, illness, debt, or other life changes can all influence an employee's decision to begin stealing, even following years of trustworthy service. Put yourself in your employee's shoes. Usually, servers and cooks make minimum wage (or slightly above). They rarely have health insurance, and they may struggle financially.

They may not be stealing cash—they may be taking food home to feed their families. This may make it easier for them to justify the theft:

"I'm not **stealing**; they throw away tons of food every night!"

Establish an open-door policy for employees to come to you. Maybe they need to request more hours. Maybe they are asking for a raise. Listen to them, even if you cannot afford to comply. Try to be understanding and flexible, especially for an employee who has given you years of valuable service.

Free employee meals are a great employee morale booster. In my restaurants, all the cooks, dishwashers, and other kitchen staff are entitled to a free meal during their shift.

When employees come in to eat on their time off, offer a generous discount for them to eat with their families. It is a good confidence booster and an easy perk that you can provide to make them feel welcome.

Remember that disgruntled employees are more likely to steal. Examine the overall mood of your staff. Are they happy and content with their jobs, or do you have serious employee turnover? If it's the latter, the problem most likely lies with management. Happy employees will often stay in low-paying jobs if they feel they are appreciated and taken care of. And high wages will not keep an employee who is miserable every day. Try to monitor the emotional climate in your kitchen.

Keep Your Nose in Everything

Be nosy. Put on an apron and heavy gloves, and go through the trash. Employees will be impressed that you are not afraid to get dirty, and it shows them that you mean business.

Have the staff throw waste in clear bins. Monitor the bins and spot check them periodically. Give incentives and rewards to staff members who perform better than others.

One strategy is to talk openly with your staff about your food costs. Tell them that food savings directly impact their salaries. Give them weekly goals and a monthly target. If they reach the target, give them a bonus. Monthly bonuses, rather than quarterly, give the employees a frequent incentive to do well.

Invest in a Good Door Alarm

I can't stress this point enough—you need to have a door alarm. Not only to protect yourself from in-house theft, but also to protect your employees from break-ins and other harm. A good door alarm system is a deterrent for theft if it is used religiously. It's not an inconvenience, and it could save your life!

Detex's customer service is very good, and they have FREE technical phone support Monday through Friday. This alone is worth the price, because so few companies even bother to offer technical support over the phone these days—they just want you to read through a 700-page manual, and leave them alone.

But don't take my word for it. You owe it to your restaurant to price-shop and find the best door alarm company for you. Take the time to research a few companies and compare price and features. Make sure that the company has a good track record, and don't be afraid to ask for customer referrals.

Sometimes the alarm can be built into a panic device, where the exit device does several jobs: locking the door while providing immediate exit during an emergency as well as an alarm that alerts staff that an unauthorized exit has occurred. Traditionally used on back doors and side doors to prevent employee thefts, many restaurants are beginning to use these products on front doors too. The alarmed exit device should have **three positions:**

- Unlocked, allowing push / pull operation without any alarm, obviously used during business hours.
- Locked from the pull side, but free exit without alarm as patrons exit the restaurant - used at closing time, while the final customers finish.
- Locked from the pull side and alarmed from the inside—used after closing and the last customer has left.

Most restaurants operate using only the first two, but in a location where staff and bartenders clean up after the last customer has left, you will find that this creates a prime theft opportunity for **dishonest employees**.

Here's the scenario: while the manager is in the kitchen or office area preparing the nightly deposit—liquor, beer, and food items can easily be taken out the front door. The alarm on the front door can not only alert management that an employee has opened a door after hours, preventing theft, but can also prevent a deadly situation from occurring.

Lack of light and maximum amount of money makes the close of business a prime time for armed robberies. Armed robbers will knock on the front door and the hostess, trying to help them find their "lost cell phone," will push the exit device and open the door, thus letting in a potential threat to everyone in the restaurant. When used properly, an after-hours front door alarm can be a very helpful tool in preventing theft in more ways than one.

Sometimes the alarm is mounted on the wall and does not lock the door, but simply monitors the door and sounds when someone exits in an unauthorized manner. When using a stand-alone exit alarm, there would obviously need to be a secondary device that would lock the door.

Outdoor exit alarms are perfect for gates on outdoor patios, helping control and direct foot traffic and back kitchen doors that are frequently sprayed and washed down. Another area is the back service gate area. These enclosed gated areas serve several purposes; they restrict someone with ill intentions from walking directly up to the back door, they provide a storage area that is protected from thieves, and they prevent crooked employees from walking out the back door and taking that box of lobsters to their car.[10]

---

[10] Ken Kuehler, Detex Corporation, used with permission.

Interview with the Safety Expert

Ken Kuehler
Detex Corporation
302 Detex Drive
New Braunfels, Texas 78130
1-800-729-3839
www.detex.com
sales@detex.com

Why don't you tell us a little bit about Detex?

Ken: Detex Corporation manufactures security hardware products, such as door alarms, panic bars, and exit alarms. These products are designed primarily to control exits and entries in commercial, institutional, and educational buildings. They are designed to help control the foot traffic inside of businesses. Detex has been a part of the restaurant industry for decades and our product selection grows every year.

We want to prevent customers or employees from walking outside with stolen goods. But, in the event of an emergency, our door alarms and panic bars still allow people to get out of the building. The alarm will sound, but in a life-safety situation, it still allows people to get out safely.

I understand that your company has developed a new alarm specifically with input from the restaurant community.

Ken: Several restaurants helped us design the new alarm. We spent quite a bit of time in California with a distributor and a large fast food chain, which helped us develop the new alarm.

What was the main concern for restaurants? Was it theft, or employee safety?

Ken: Well, the restaurant industry actually came to us, and they wanted something that was going to help them operationally. They wanted something that would help secure the back door, as well as curtail the risk of armed robbery. In the restaurant industry, if the back door is propped open, you are more vulnerable to armed robbery. It's a real fear in the restaurant industry.

The owners still need to use that back door to receive goods, take out trash, etc. But at the same time, owners don't want to leave the door propped open longer than necessary. That was the challenge that these restaurants came to us with—they needed something that would prevent an alarm bypass for an extended period. On the new alarm, you set a time on it, so that the door cannot remain open for an indefinite period.

Your new design was created with restaurant input, correct?

Ken: Well, restaurant managers are so busy—they have to deal with their customers, the kitchen, and a slew of other duties. Managers are constantly floating. So, if the back door has to be open, and the manager can't be there 100 percent of the time, this timed bypass alarm will allow you to prop the door open for five minutes or ten minutes.

Depending on what management wants to do, it allows managers to leave the back door unattended for short periods. The door alarm will sound if the door is left open for longer than the timer setting. If the task is completed within the time period on the alarm timer, then the door alarm will automatically reset, so the manager doesn't have to come back with the key. It saves a lot of hassles.

Compliance seems to be the biggest issue for managers. WE are so busy all the time. It's always a challenge to be everywhere at once.

Ken: Yes, The biggest problem restaurants have with back doors is really compliance.

So we developed an alarm that allowed managers to set a timer so they could walk away and not leave the door propped open indefinitely. This is called our Timed Bypass Alarm. We designed it with the input of restaurants in order to help managers regulate the amount of time the back door is left open.

I mean, we understand—the kitchen is hot and noisy, and there is a desire to open that back door and let in some fresh air. Employees also like to step out back, to smoke, cool off, or take a break, but that's when you really open yourself up to an armed robbery—it can turn deadly if the owners are not careful.

This is the main reason why we developed this type of alarm. We have a few store retailers using it, but it was primarily designed for the restaurant industry.

Everyone hears about those restaurant horror stories where employees are injured or threatened during an armed robbery. But a lot of theft is also perpetrated by employees.

Ken: Yes, we have restaurant customers that place door alarms not only on the back doors and side doors, but also the front door. The front door exit alarm is used in a totally different way.

During regular business hours, it allows people to come and go, but after hours, it doesn't allow anyone to exit the door without sounding an alarm. So, in an emergency, all the employees could exit the building, but it prevents two things: it prevents employees from taking stolen products out, and it prevents someone from coming in after-hours that might have criminal intentions.

As for armed robberies during the day, there's always a risk that there will be an armed robbery through the front door, but the door alarms are designed to be a deterrent when restaurants are most venerable. There are other products, such as camera systems, that can be helpful deterrents to robbery during regular business hours.

In varying degrees, almost all restaurants experience some type of employee theft. What do you think owners can do to help control this problem?

Ken: Well, managers should **always** do a closing walk-through to make sure the restaurant perimeter is secure. The front of the restaurant is usually a well-monitored area, but more often than not, what we see is a **dishonest employee** that takes items out the back door. They either take the item out and hide it in the trash and retrieve it later, or take it directly to their car after closing. It's so important to have a back door alarm, and to use it correctly.

Do you have any stories where a customer has discovered a theft after installing an alarm?

Ken: Yes, one restaurant chain that installed front door alarms discovered rampant employee theft after-hours. The restaurant originally had just a turn-key lock on the front door. The manager was usually in the office doing the deposit, and the rest of the staff was supposed to be busy cleaning and doing their closing duties. But they discovered that bottles of liquor were disappearing into the parking lot and into employees' cars. The manager was unaware that this was going on, and it was only discovered after the front door alarm was installed.

It's a problem in the retail industry, too. Most restaurants will install an alarm on the back door, but forget the alarm on the front door. The manager generally won't open the back door until he's done doing the deposit. It's sad, but the employees will just estimate how long that takes, and it only takes the employee about a minute to walk out to their car with stolen goods.

We take calls all day long from restaurant owners with similar stories.

Commandment #6: Strive for Perfect Sanitation

"A mass of insects is incompatible with creating guest comfort and enthusiasm."

-Bill Marvin, Restaurant Basics

A Clean Kitchen Prevents Pests

In general, anything that comes into contact with fresh produce has the potential to contaminate it. Most of the food safety issues we face are straightforward. 90 percent of the toughest sanitation issues a chef faces revolve around these three problems.

- Temperature control
- Personal hygiene
- Cross-contamination [11]

While the food supply in the United States is one of the safest in the world, the U.S. Centers for Disease Control and Prevention (CDC) estimates that 76 million people get sick, more than 300,000 are hospitalized, and 5,000 Americans die each year from food-borne illness.[12] Don't let your kitchen become one of these statistics!

The Buck Stops with You!

The CDC says that the most common causes of food-borne illness are:

- Inadequate cooling and cold holding,
- Preparing food too far ahead of service,
- Inadequate reheating and inadequate hot holding,
- Poor personal hygiene or infected personnel
- Contaminated raw foods & ingredients

If you concentrate your food safety program on these common mistakes, you are already ahead of the game. A clean kitchen and healthy personnel are essential to a chef's success,

---

[11] Food Safety: The 90% Rule. Christopher Meier, AVP Operations, Ecolab

[12] Department of Health and Human Services, Centers for Disease Control, www.cdc.gov/foodsafety

and it is your ultimate responsibility to make sure that your kitchen is safe, clean, and free of disease. You are the Chef—and **the Buck Stops with <u>You!</u>**

Everyone knows that a clean kitchen helps prevent pests, such as rodents and insects. A single cockroach sighting in your restaurant can cause a customer to "spread the word" about how unclean your restaurant is. And I have a little secret for you that most chefs already know: *every restaurant* has pests, whether you can see them or not. It's your job to get rid of them.

You have to stay on top of your pest management program at all times. Can you imagine a mouse running through your dining room on a busy Saturday night? One frightened scream of "mouse!" could kill your business for good. The sad part is that some restaurant owners are completely ambivalent to the problem.

A regular sanitation program is a great way to reduce food-borne illness, and prevent pests from making your kitchen their home.

Most restaurant chains invest in regular (professional) pest management. Regular inspections and visits from a pest control service help reduce the risk of infestation and the possibility that a customer will find insects or other pests in the restaurant and in their food.

Pest control visits usually take place a minimum of once a month. Twice a month is industry standard, especially for the larger chains and franchises. If you cannot afford monthly pest control, you may be able to do some of the pest management yourself. But the laws in each state are strict and there are many chemicals that are unsafe or illegal to use around food.

Restaurant owners and managers must be aware that although in most states they can do their own pest control, there are strict regulations for pest management in any commercial food handling area. Many insecticides are unsafe to use around food, and the laws are even stricter for rodent removal. The state and federal regulations exist in order to ensure that food, food preparation equipment, serving areas, etc. are not contaminated with pesticide, insecticide, or rodenticide residues.

The insecticides used for homes are not always appropriate for use in commercial kitchens due to possible contamination of foods and utensils. Real care must be taken in choosing the correct products for sensitive areas.

Never apply insecticides while food is being prepared, served, eaten or otherwise open or exposed. [13] If you have any questions about the legality of the chemicals you are using—don't use them! Instead, contact your local pest control company and ask for a consultation. A pest inspector will usually meet with you for free, and you can ask for recommendations on how to keep your kitchen area pest-free.

Controlling Flies in Your Restaurant

The very nature of food preparation increases the problems of indoor and outdoor flies. Most restaurants have at least a minor problem with flies. The doors open, patrons come in, and the flies sneak in, too. This is the "minor" problem.

---

[13] Pest Control. Restaurant Pest Control. www.pestproducts.com.

Major problems with flies (and maggots) occur when restaurants do a poor job of controlling where flies breed and reproduce. Restaurants cannot ignore fly populations and the danger to health and safety that they cause. This goes back to the issue of controlling food waste. Food waste is the main attractant for flies and other unwelcome outdoor pests. If you can control your food waste using innovative methods, then you will have an easier time controlling flies.

Keep outdoor areas as clean as possible. Waste containers must be kept covered. Dumpsters and garbage disposal equipment must be kept clean, and sprayed out after every garbage pick-up, or maggots and flies will breed in the scraps that are left behind by the garbage truck.

Garbage duty is unpleasant work. You must make sure the employees are doing their jobs. Remind employees about dumpster procedures; keeping the back dock area clean and always closing the dumpster lid after use.

For persistent problems with flies, roaches, and ants, a good pest control and prevention plan is needed. Your pest company must also spray exterior doors and walls near garbage containers.

For indoor flies, you can install professional ultraviolet fly traps. Fly zappers should **never** be used in food handling areas. For sensitive kitchen areas a fly trap that uses a combination of ultraviolet and pheromones is best. A good pest control company can recommend fly traps that are applicable for use in a kitchen setting. Recently, I've seen "fancy" ultraviolet traps that are designed to be part of the décor, even in the dining area.

Rodent Removal and Control

For rodent removal, get a professional pest company to help you. Do not attempt to trap the rodents yourself, and do not touch them. They can harbor disease and parasites even after they are dead.

Rodent removal in restaurants is a very sensitive issue. It is illegal and unsafe to use snap traps or rodenticides in any area where food is being prepared or served. Never use any rodent control item that might contaminate food or utensils with baits, poisons, or rodent body parts. Using rat poison anywhere around the restaurant can be unsafe for dogs, children, and wild birds.

Using tamper-resistant bait stations on the exterior is very important. Outdoor bait boxes keep rodent baits and traps safe from non-target animals such as cats and birds, and they give you a chance to kill the rodents before they have a chance to enter the kitchen. If there are guard dogs or other non-target animals or wildlife nearby, tamper-resistant bait stations are a must.

The only acceptable devices to use indoors are glue traps and live traps. These items will help capture rats or mice that manage to get into the building. The best results are always achieved by stopping rodents before they even enter your kitchen. Keep dumpsters as clean as possible; cut grass and weeds along fence rows where rodents might hide or build their nests.

When in doubt about any pest management procedure or installation of pest control devices, you must always check with your pest management company. Defer to their expertise, or you may find yourself in hot water you're your local authorities. The health and welfare of your customers should be of paramount concern. [14]

Institute a Cleaning Program

The first step toward perfect sanitation is regular cleaning. Make sure all your cooks understand the importance of cleanliness, and the possible repercussions of a bad Health Department review (loss of hours, raises, customers, or restaurant closure). Cleaning should be done throughout the day. Closing duties must always include a thorough cleaning of the kitchen. Deep cleaning of the kitchen, including walls, stainless steel, and other hard-to-reach areas should happen at least once a week.

Regular cleaning is essential to any restaurant's success. Even if you are lucky enough to afford a night crew, the cooks must always perform their closing duties, which include cleaning the kitchen. If cleaning is not regular and diligent, your kitchen will become the favorite dining place for cockroaches, rather than people!

In smaller kitchens, the kitchen staff is usually required to do the nightly clean-up. Once of the biggest reasons for kitchen staff turnover is the requirement for the regular kitchen staff to do the nightly clean up duty. Cleaning duties can be incredibly demoralizing at the end of a long night. If at all possible, try to hire a nightly clean-up crew, or else you may lose more money training new cooks to replace your exhausted ones.

This doesn't mean that the cooks cannot do on-the-job cleaning during their shift—on the contrary, cleaning should

---

[14] www.pestproducts.com/restaurants

occur throughout the shift. And deep cleaning can happen on a schedule; such as once a week. But nightly clean up is extremely difficult after a full shift, and is especially hard on the cooks on weekends.

Organize your pantry and coolers to prevent spilling, dripping, or cross-contamination. Buy cleaning supplies designed for commercial kitchens. NEVER keep cleaning supplies near food supplies, or in the pantry near dry goods. The smell from bleach or ammonia can permeate vegetables and other delicate foods, making them unfit to eat.

Train your staff, step-by-step, on the proper use of cleaning supplies and chemicals. Kitchen staff really appreciate it when the head chef isn't afraid to get his hands dirty every once in a while, too. Let your staff know that a clean restaurant is as important to your success as the food they produce every day.

Always use a cleaning checklist. In addition to daily cleaning, you should schedule a heavy-duty clean-up no less than once a month. Make it mandatory, and make sure the servers, cooks, and support staff all participate. Make sure you have a Master Cleaning Schedule and assign employees to specific jobs. Rotate employees, and commend them when they do a good job.

Keep trash bins as far away from the building as possible, and always keep the bins sealed. Ask your waste disposal company for regular bin cleaning and rotation to prevent pests.

Make sure all of your employees have good direction from you, in writing, about how and when they are supposed to clean. Your staff will take their cues from you, so make sure you set a good example and give constructive criticism when warranted.

Super-Quick Cleaning Tips

Save time with quick tips to keep your kitchen gleaming.

1. You can shine your appliances using rubbing alcohol, and you can clean water spots from stainless steel by soaking a cloth in rubbing alcohol and then wiping the spots away.
2. To quickly clean a drink or bar blender, fill it two-thirds with hot water, add a drop or two of dish soap, and then turn it on. Rinse well before the next use.
3. Run a piece of bread through your meat grinder before washing in order to loosen particles.
4. For grease clogs in your sink, try pouring one cup of salt and one cup of baking soda into the drain. Follow this with BOILING hot water.
5. Lemons are your friend. Lemons remove fish and garlic odors from skin, cutting boards, and even your hair! You can use half a lemon down a smelly bar garbage disposal to eliminate odors without a bleach smell, which customers dislike.

Preventing Food-borne Illness

Over 75 percent of consumers believe food-related illness is a serious threat to their health. Many believe the threat is greater today than in the past.

Basic food protection practices related to worker health and hygiene fall into two categories: disease control and cleanliness. Workers carry microbes on their skin, in their hair, on their hands, and in their digestive systems or respiratory tracts.

Restaurant employees must:

1. Maintain adequate personal cleanliness.
2. Wash hands frequently.
3. Change disposable gloves whenever contamination is a possibility.
4. Wear appropriate clothing on the job. The FDA recommends that employees wear clean clothes and any additional outer items (e.g., hairnets and beard covers, lab coats, aprons, and appropriate footwear)
5. Employees must not eat, use tobacco, chew gum, or spit in the kitchen.

* **Work from top down** for cleaning and sanitizing activities. Some equipment may need to be disassembled before cleaning and sanitizing followed by reassembly.

A chef should post pictorial representations of good practices covered in training. I recommend that signs be multilingual and posted in conspicuous places where food will be prepared. [15]

Preventing food-borne illness and death remains a major public health challenge. All good chefs must institute the highest level of sanitation procedures. At the beginning, sanitation procedures may seem a bit cumbersome or time consuming, but nothing is as important to your kitchen's success as cleanliness.

Next is an example of a "training aid" on cleaning and sanitizing steps within processing areas. You should always

---

[15] U.S. Department of Health and Human Services. Guide to Minimize Microbial Food Safety Hazards of Fresh-cut Fruits and Vegetables, 2007

have a checklist that's plainly visible for cooks to see. This helps them remember the steps, even after a long night.[16]

Cleaning and sanitizing steps

1. Remove heavy debris from floors with brooms or shovels and dry clean processing equipment, if needed
2. Pre-rinse the equipment with adequate quality water
3. Clean remaining debris from floor
4. Rinse floor and drains with adequate quality water using a low pressure hose
5. Use dedicated brushes to scrub floor and drains
6. Foam and scrub the equipment with an effective cleaner
7. Thoroughly rinse the equipment, floors, and drains with adequate quality water using a low pressure hose
8. Remove excess water from floors
9. Sanitize (according to manufacturer directions) the equipment and floors

One bad experience with the Health department can ruin a restaurant's reputation forever. In California, where Health Department reviews are required to be posted conspicuously, a "yellow card" is equivalent to the kiss of death. A "red card" means immediate closure.

Although sanitation costs may seem high at first, the potential cost savings are enormous, especially considering the fact that a bad score can close down your kitchen indefinitely!

---

[16] U.S. Department of Health and Human Services. Guide to Minimize Microbial Food Safety Hazards of Fresh-cut Fruits and Vegetables, 2007

Servsafe™ Certification

I recommend that all chefs and restaurant owners receive at the minimum a Servsafe™ certification, and also require all their managers, supervisors, and even lead hourly employees to do the same. A Servsafe program will teach your key employees about:

1. Basic food safety
2. Personal hygiene
3. Cross-contamination & allergens
4. Time & temperature
5. Cleaning & sanitation

A little education can save you thousands of dollars in the long run by preventing food-borne illness (do ***you*** want to deal with a customer lawsuit?). Prevention is the key![17]

Posting the Servsafe certificate in a public place looks good too, especially for smaller establishments. It shows a dedication to maintaining a standard of cleanliness and food safety.

Restaurant owners and chefs are responsible for ensuring that their employees are in good health and not at risk for transmitting a food-borne illness. In California and in some other states, restaurant operators are now required to designate a key employee or "person in charge" during all hours of operation. Consequently, employees are required to report if they are diagnosed with a reportable illness.

Restrict sick employees from working with unpackaged food, clean equipment, utensils, and linens if the employee is suffering from symptoms of gastrointestinal illness or has

---

[17] ServSafe *Starters*™ Program, www.servsafe.com

persistent coughing and sneezing that cannot be controlled by medication. (The chef may remove the restriction once the employee no longer has any symptoms of illness).

Ensure that any employees with open sores on their hands or wrists bandage the sores and wear single-use gloves over the bandage. The employee must change the gloves every time they would be required to wash their hands.

Train all employees to be knowledgeable regarding the relationship between personal hygiene, employee health, and food safety.

Commandment #7: Cut Labor Costs and Other Kitchen Costs

"Small business owners should not be afraid to introduce pay cuts to bring wages more in line with the competition. Employees may be more sympathetic to a well-explained pay cut than to layoffs."

-Caroline Foster, Small Business News

Institute a Labor-Saving Program

High daily labor costs can cripple a restaurant, and a high turnover rate can do the same, by forcing the chef or the owners to continually train new employees at an escalating cost. Cooks typically have the highest wages in the restaurant, other than management. In the kitchen, it is absolutely essential that the chef learns how to manage labor.

Most managers agree that labor costs are the most difficult issue before them. It is easier to control food and beverage costs through menu price adjustments, and smarter food ordering. However, labor costs cannot be controlled using the same techniques.

Everyone knows that the restaurant industry has a notorious reputation for staff turnover and human resource difficulties. Remember that a large part of employee retention and productivity relates to job satisfaction, and that has to come from **you**. Employees must be given strong direction, constructive but not humiliating criticism, as well as respect and appreciation.

Good restaurant employees are always in short supply, and all owners are faced with the same dilemma—walking the labor dollars tightrope!

- **Pay low wages?** Lose your best staff to higher-paying competitors.
- **Pay high wages?** Lose your profit margin to out of control labor costs, including wages, employment taxes, and workers compensation costs.

It's an impossible situation! The best way to manage labor costs is through smart scheduling techniques, employee rewards programs, and extensive cross-training. You can also save labor dollars if you invest in labor-saving equipment.

You have to recognize and track your labor costs over time, recognize the employees that give you the best reliability and productivity, and distinguish where you can maximize employee productivity.

You can institute a more effective labor-saving program in about ten days and re-organize your kitchen for maximum efficiency. Here are the first steps:

1. Rate Your Staff from Strongest to Weakest. Use your most recent monthly schedule, and go down the line. Be as objective as possible, and rate your staff based on skills and reliability. Do you have a cook that arrives late every day, but is a superstar on the line? Do you have a reliable cook that is weak on the grill, but strong at the salad station?

Rate each employee so you can see their value to your bottom line in black and white. Use a weighted average. Indentify employees that are more valuable and reliable. Then it is easier to assign raises and you have a paper trail and good notes as an explanation for an employee who is denied a raise because of work performance.

Employees need direction, and you need to be the one to provide it. Do quarterly employee evaluations, and take the time to tell employees how they are doing in writing. If you have a great employee that changes shifts a lot (even with good reason), let him/her know that it makes it harder for you to schedule shifts when there are other employees who are more reliable and work just as hard.

2. Cross Train, Cross Train, and Cross Train Some More! The more cooks, dishwashers, and prep staff you have cross-trained, the better! Cross-training your staff will take lots of time and effort, but it's worth it! Having a dishwasher that can jump in and prep a much-needed item on a busy Friday night is a godsend.

Train your best cooks on every station. Even a few hours of extra training can make a huge difference when you are short-staffed, or one of your best cooks calls in sick.

3. Use a Scheduling Program. Don't just try to track your schedules in Excel! Unless all your employees are family members and don't mind constant scheduling mishaps and conflicts, I recommend that you invest in professional software to track your scheduling and labor hours. Watch your percentages, adjust labor needs weekly, and make sure you are giving your best employees the hours that they need. Good software is worth every penny when you are trying to cut costs and still manage labor efficiently.

4. Reward Staff Members. Always reward your best staff members. Let them know that they are appreciated. Your employees are your best asset; every employee is an investment in training and labor dollars in order to produce a return. Your best staff should get the best schedules and the highest wages. Give perks and recognition to your best performers. Sometimes even a small reward, such as movie tickets or a gift card, can produce real loyalty and employee satisfaction.

Stop Long Ticket Times

Long ticket times are a common problem in restaurants, and nothing will scare a potential regular customer away like having to wait 45 minutes or more to get their food. There are many factors that can increase ticket times. But one of the most common problems starts when a chef overloads one kitchen station.

Part of designing a menu that works is making sure you are not overloading one station in the kitchen, or one piece of equipment. Your menu needs to be designed with your kitchen's labor and equipment constraints in mind. Here are some tips.

1. Create a graph showing which kitchen station prepares each menu item. Within that graph, list each piece of equipment necessary for the production of each item.
2. Balance menu items between each kitchen station and each piece of equipment within the stations.
3. Eliminate or modify menu items that require production in more than two stations.

It really can be as simple as that. With the graph as a visual tool, it's easy to see if you have overloaded a particular station. Chefs have a propensity to do so based on their own tastes or experience cooking particular dishes.

Remember, you only have one chance to make a good first impression. Work out details like this before you open your doors, or you'll be closing them a lot sooner than you want to.

Observe, Identify and Re-demonstrate

One of the primary reasons that training programs work is in the method their managers and trainers use to teach new skills.

This seems to be especially true in restaurants and food services due to the prevalence of managers without any formal teaching education or training.

While proper teaching technique is not something that comes naturally to everyone, it is easy to learn following a simple, multi-step procedure.

- Write procedures on paper for whatever skill is being taught. Always have written instructions.
- In the kitchen, it is usually helpful to have the instructions in English and Spanish. Distribute these written procedures to all the employees being trained.
- Review the written procedure with the employees.
- Ask if anyone has questions. Answer any questions or concerns about the procedure.
- Confirm the person's comprehension.
- Demonstrate the procedure to the employee. Then, observe the employee demonstrating the procedure to you.
- Identify any wrong steps in the person's procedure.
- Re-demonstrate the procedure using the correct method.
- Repeat the "Observe, Identify and Re-demonstrate" steps until the person is able to perform the procedure without errors at least three consecutive times.
- Reward employees with praise when they perform the procedure correctly.

This method will work to teach most skills or processes, but you must have the patience to repeat the "Observe, Identify and Re-demonstrate" steps until your employee has mastered the skill. As with anything, practice makes perfect!

This technique should not only be used to teach new skills, but also to correct any procedures performed incorrectly by an employee. Steadfast resolve by managers to use this technique will result in greater compliance by employees.

Understand Your Sales Volume

The most effective method of managing labor costs is first understanding your sales volume. Adjust your staff levels for busier periods. Lower your staff levels for slower days. Understand the local employee laws as they apply in your state.

Find out if you are required to pay an employee if they come into the restaurant and they are not needed. Keep track of your labor costs and your sales from year to year—this is especially helpful for tracking those surprise busy days because of regional events.

You can then make an assessment of how many employees you need for a given shift, with certain adjustments for holidays and special events. Keep good sales records from year to year; it will get easier and easier as time goes on. But be diligent and recognize that your labor needs will change with different environmental and economic conditions.

Don't Get Bombed!

I am the chef and owner of a small Italian restaurant. Last year, we got absolutely SLAMMED one Monday night in the middle of April. I wasn't prepared for it and I ended up running long ticket times and comping a lot of meals.

It was a local soccer tournament and I was totally unprepared. The following year, I had the foresight to contact the soccer event coordinators and get the tournament date. I was told that they were having food booths, as well. We decided to participate and represent our restaurant at the event. So I made sure the restaurant was fully staffed, and I even went out personally to the event to set up a food booth. My wife and kids staffed the food booth, and my best employees helped me run the restaurant that day. Everyone worked a double-shift!

I went back and forth between the event and the restaurant the entire day. By the end of the night, I was exhausted—but what a great day! We tripled our regular sales figures, plus the additional sales at the tournament. And we handed out menus, flyers, and "lunch loyalty cards," which invited people to come in for our lunch specials. The day was a great success—and all because I took the time to pull last year's calendar and tried to figure out "what went wrong" that Monday night a year ago!

Save on Utility Costs

The kitchen is the largest energy drain in the restaurant. You can reduce overhead costs by implementing energy-saving techniques.

Use cut-off switches for the air conditioning. Make sure it's on a timer so that it doesn't get left on at night, which is a huge energy waste. Put your lights on motion sensors too, especially in outdoor areas and the dry storage, and any other places that are used infrequently.

Change your lighting to fluorescent lighting wherever possible. Sodium lighting is a cost-efficient option for outdoor lighting.

Change stoves from electricity to natural gas. Natural gas is generally the cheaper option for stoves, air conditioning, and water heating. Replace oven seals and refrigerator seals frequently. If you can afford it, consider solar panels for hot water heating. Solar panels usually recover their installation costs within five to eight years. After that, it's all cost savings.

Consider using a microwave for some cooking and thawing tasks. Thawing food with hot water is not only unsafe, it's also expensive.

Commandment # 8: Introduce a Special Menu

"Adding a separate menu shows a commitment to a targeted group."

-Gregg Rapp, Menu Engineer

There are many types of special menus that you can create to generate revenue. Writing a special menu can be fun. You can play around with different menu items and see what ends up being more profitable.

Make sure that you watch your food costs and portion control closely on your Special Menu offerings, especially for discounted items like Happy Hour specials. You still need to make a profit, but you also need to be competitive with your local market.

Every **Special Menu** is targeted to a specific audience, and some are more profitable than others. Some good examples of "special menus" are:

1. A "Late Night" menu
2. A senior menu
3. Daily specials (as an insert to a regular menu)
4. Bar or Happy Hour menu
5. Special Events menu/catering
6. A dietary menu

Make sure your most profitable items are highlighted on each special menu.

Senior Menu

A senior menu is a good way to offer smaller portions and lower prices to a targeted audience. Seniors can be an untapped market—they typically eat earlier, so they don't interfere with your late night rush, and they are good customers overall (no "dine and dash" problems). They also become steady regulars. Seniors are often on fixed incomes or Social Security, and they look for bargains.

If you want to attract seniors, consider adding a senior menu, and offering a selection of your regular menu items. Offer all of the items at a fixed price, say $6.95. Make the portions smaller and the choices limited. It's a good way to attract an early crowd with very little effort.

Many restaurants offer senior discounts, rather than a full menu. Some offer free coffee, early bird discounts, or coupons specifically targeted to seniors. Some operators are reluctant to offer senior menus because of age sensitivity, especially with female patrons. Some restaurants will not offer a senior menu unless it is specifically requested by the guest.

Usually, senior offerings are made to patrons age fifty or older. Most regional chains offer senior discounts at sixty or older.

Late Night Menu

Late night menus can be a highly profitable option for many restaurants. If your establishment is close to movie theaters or nightclubs, and you are open late, consider offering a "late night" menu.

Hungry club and bar patrons are an untapped market segment in most cities, as are servers and bartenders from other restaurants who are looking to unwind.

By offering a late night menu, you are filling a niche. Late night menus also have the added benefit of increasing liquor and beer sales as well.

The dishes should be low cost, quick, and easy food items that allow you to have fewer cooks and servers on staff. Some restaurants have instituted "Industry Night," which is an evening during the week where servers, bartenders, and cooks from other restaurants can eat at a discounted rate.

Money in the Bank

In Ohio, The Cocktails Lounge offers restaurant workers deep discounts every Sunday night. Discounts are offered to anyone wearing a restaurant uniform.

Servers and cooks from other restaurants go there for $2 draft beer and half-price appetizers until closing time. Local word-of-mouth has spread. Servers and bartenders from dozens of local restaurants go there to unwind, relax, and spend some of their hard-earned dollars after their shifts. Because of this, The Cocktails Lounge has a bustling Sunday night business, which is usually the slowest night of the week for most restaurants.

Hot wings, quesadillas, mozzarella sticks, onion rings, nachos, and other fried foods are all staples of the late night menu. If your chef can prepare another signature item quickly and inexpensively, consider adding it to your late night menu as well.

Happy Hour Menu

A Happy Hour menu can increase sales in any establishment, even if you don't have a bar. A Happy Hour menu is specifically designed to bring customers into the restaurant during slower periods such as the early afternoon. You can choose to offer food specials, drink specials, or both.

Make sure that your menu items still turn a decent profit. A good example of high-margin items that can usually be deeply discounted are:

- Small pizzas
- Draft beer
- Well drinks
- Pre-blended margaritas
- Hot wings
- French fries (basket)
- Chili fries
- Onion rings
- Stuffed mushrooms
- Crab cakes (imitation crab)
- Fried calamari
- Mozzarella sticks
- Potato skins

You can create a "Sampler Platter" or a variety platter of a selection of these items for your Happy Hour patrons. Sampler platters are always a big hit with groups, and it often encourages higher liquor sales.

These are all high-margin items that you can offer to your customers and still make money. Display your Happy Hour menu on table tents or a smaller bar menu. You can also use a dry-erase board and change your Happy Hour specials every week. This creates variety and can drive customers to your restaurant.

Daily Specials

Offering a daily special can be a nice way to vary your menu and set yourself apart from other restaurants in the area. It's also a time-honored way to reduce the risk of spoilage from items that have a short shelf life, like fresh fish, shellfish, and fresh meats. Customers expect to pay more for signature dishes, so it's a great way to increase your price points without affecting your regular menu or surprising customers.

Sales have been shown to increase by 15 percent for restaurants that offer daily or weekly specials. Use highlight boxes, and make sure your servers mention the specials. Specials should all be written down as an insert to your regular menu.

Dietary Menus

There's big dollars in dietary menus, as many restaurants have already discovered. A dietary menu is any menu that is specifically targeted towards customers who have specific dietary needs, such as a Kosher, Vegan, or a Gluten-free menu. The dietary needs may be religious, lifestyle, or health-related. Look at your local populace. Is there a huge demand for natural foods and vegetarian items in your community? Then consider adding a strict vegan menu.

More and more Americans are diagnosed with celiac disease every year. The cure for this disease is a completely gluten-free diet. Gluten is a type of protein found in wheat, rye, and barley. Gluten is commonly used in animal and human foods, and is even found in some cosmetics.

Nielsen Co., which tracks gluten-free food in the U.S., reported that the gluten-free sector increased 20 percent from 2007 to 2008, to $1.75 billion from $1.46 billion a year ago.[18] That's a huge increase. Think about ways that you can add a dietary menu to your restaurant. It's a great way to increase a "niche" customer base with very little effort.

The Gluten Intolerance Group of North America offers a service known as the *Gluten-Free Restaurant Awareness Program.* They list all the restaurants that offer a gluten-free menu. If you have a newsletter, then you could announce that you have decided to add gluten-free items to your menu, as well. The Macaroni Grill and the Lone Star Steakhouse already offer gluten-free items, and offer suggestions on their menu for those with gluten sensitivities.

Gluten-free desserts are especially difficult to prepare, because removing wheat from recipes changes the texture. But you can outsource this task by purchasing excellent gluten-free desserts and charging a premium for them. If you enjoy baking, you can experiment with different types of starches in order to get the texture and flavors that you like. The development of a popular specialty dessert can make your restaurant a Mecca for people who are looking for tasty solutions to their dietary problems.

Joshua Short is the executive pastry chef of Buzz Bakery in Alexandria, Virginia. He has created a huge customer following by developing his famous "Bird Brownie". Josh

[18] The Glories of Gluten-Free, QSR Magazine

uses rice flour, almond flour, espresso, and walnuts to create his delicious gluten-free brownie. Can you create your own "signature" desserts for your customers?

The possibilities are endless. You can offer similar menu options for diabetics and other targeted groups. Be creative!

Commandment # 9: Increase Perceived Value

"When customers are considering value, perception can be as important as reality. Wine makers know that screw cap bottles are better and cheaper than traditional cork. Yet it is impossible to change to screw caps, because buyers equate screw caps with inferior wine."

- **Edward de Bono,** The Thinking Managers

Great Expectations

Studies show that a customer's perceived value of a restaurant directly affects their satisfaction. Perceived value is the maximum that the customer will pay for a product or service. There are many ways to increase perceived value without spending money, and sometimes making your restaurant seem more "upscale" just takes some imagination.

A restaurant's image greatly affects a customer's perception of perceived value. Numerous researchers agree that a customer's perception of a restaurant greatly affects customer satisfaction.[19] I say "perception" because reality is often far from a customer's perception.

For example, researchers found that customers' recollection of their meal price was directly tied to the level of service they received. Customers who liked the restaurant service recall paying close to what they actually paid. Customers who disliked the restaurant recall overpaying—they felt as if the meal was overpriced, or they remember the check amount as more expensive than it actually was! [20]

Surpass your guests' expectations, and you can charge more for the same dish. Service is a huge issue, and it affects your customers' perception of food value. Even in a fast-food restaurant, quick service with a smile can mean the difference between a happy return customer and a displeased one. In most cases, if the service is good, it can even make up for lesser food quality.

---

[19] Ryu, Kisang. *The Relationships Among Store Image, Perceived Value, Customer Satisfaction, and Behavioral Intentions in the Fast-Casual Restaurant Industry*. University of New Orleans, 2008.

[20] Thomas J. Kelly, Nicholas M. Kiefer, and Kenneth Burdett. *A Demand-Based Approach to Menu Pricing*, 1994.

Make Sure Your Guests Are Cozy!

Customers are picky about their seating, especially when the restaurant is not on a wait. Customers also hate to eat in empty restaurants. It makes them feel "lonely." Everyone wants to be at the "hot spot!" Be open to modifying your seating arrangements. This might drive your servers crazy at first, but try to understand that customers hate rigid seating policies.

A big, empty dining area is not appealing to guests. So organize your main dining room to feel cozier and try to seat guests there, especially at the beginning of the shift. If possible, use plants, mirrors, or temporary partitions to break up the seating areas.

People like being in a busy, "happening" restaurant, but they also like the feeling of some privacy—lower the lights in the main seating area and offer drink specials early in the evening. A good Happy Hour is a wonderful way to get guests in the restaurant and fill up those empty seats.

If you have the ability to do so, try to set up a series of semi-private areas in your restaurant that you can open up as you get busier throughout the night. Do you have an enclosed patio or a sunroom? Use it! Utilize the space for private parties during slower periods, and pack it with people on your busy nights. Keep the atmosphere inviting and warm.

Dirty Bathrooms Lower Perceived Value

Customers believe: Dirty Bathroom=Dirty Kitchen

A dirty bathroom always lowers perceived value of a restaurant. Don't bother paying for cloth napkins and tablecloths if your bathroom is dirty or outdated. Customers equate a dirty bathroom with a dirty kitchen. Even if your kitchen is spotless, if your bathroom smells dirty or chemical-like, people will think that your kitchen is also unclean. You are just throwing money in the toilet!

There is a serious lack of cleanliness in many small restaurants. Bathrooms are typically smelly and not stocked with paper towels or toilet paper. This is especially true in the women's bathrooms, and my wife is always extremely vocal about the bathroom conditions! Women hate filthy restrooms. It's often a real deal-killer for them, and they are 50 percent of the customer market.

Bathrooms in particular get overlooked in small businesses. Paint gets old and dirty. Floors are mopped with the same mop used on the greasy restaurant floors. Mirrors are broken and never fixed. The hot water doesn't work, and the towel dispensers aren't kept full. The hand soap is empty and there are no sanitary napkins or tampons in the machine in the ladies room. Strong disinfectants are used regularly to clean toilets and sinks, and the bathroom ends up smelling like a porta-potty.

The situation in the dining room isn't much better. Furniture and fixtures are in disrepair, menus have little pieces of food stuck on them, and glasses are often dirty.

Cleanliness is an area of running a restaurant that is often ignored by small restaurant owners, but ranks very high in importance to customers. Don't get complacent about cleanliness. Don't be fooled—customers notice. Their eyes go directly to the bits of food on the floor, the grimy walls, and the missing paper towels.

While you may see a bathroom as more of a necessity (and maybe a nuisance) than your customers, it's **their opinion** that matters, not yours. They have to be able to make it out of your bathroom feeling clean enough to touch bread before putting it in their mouths. Customers need to feel secure enough to sit down in your bathroom and not feel disgusted.

One thing that independent restaurant owners can learn from big chains is how to keep a clean bathroom. McDonald's has one person on every shift designated to keep the bathrooms clean. The designated employee makes hourly bathroom checks. They clean up excess water. Mop up any "spills." Replenish soap. Empty the trash. Make sure paper towel dispensers are full. They wipe down dirty toilets if necessary, and basically do everything they can to make sure their customers know they will always have a clean, stocked restroom to use.

A very successful regional convenience store named **Quiktrip** also applies this philosophy. Their bathrooms are always clean, and they are rewarded with residual business from people stopping to use the bathroom. This policy builds respect from their customers, and a reputation as a clean, upstanding company. Ask yourself these questions:

- Is there plenty of toilet paper in my bathrooms?
- How about paper towels and soap?
- Do my bathrooms smell?
- Is there build-up on sinks or toilets?
- Are the bathroom walls clean?
- Are there holes in the walls or ceilings? Are there missing tiles in the ceiling or on the floor?
- Is anything in the bathroom broken?
- Is there graffiti on walls or stalls?

- When is the last time the bathroom was painted?
- Are the colors and finishes attractive?
- Do my toilets and/or urinals leak?
- Is there ever standing water on the floor?
- Do the doors lock when they're supposed to?
- Do my bathrooms offer enough privacy for each individual in the bathroom stall?
- How often do I have the bathrooms checked on?
- Is there an employee on every shift assigned to keep the bathrooms clean and stocked?

Answering these questions and remedying the situation immediately should produce bathrooms that even the pickiest customer will be satisfied with. Do whatever it takes. Your efforts will be rewarded with happier customers.

Commandment #10: Offer Private Banquets and Catering

"There is definite opportunity for great wealth within the catering field. Anyone with a sense of service to others can succeed."

-Business Ideas Directory

Catering

A great way to increase sales is to offer catering services, which are essentially just larger portions of your existing dishes. Catering and banquet services can really boost your bottom line because much of the guesswork that goes along with your regular dinner guests is taken out of the equation.

Banquets and catering services have highly controllable costs (a chef's dream!). Usually, the kitchen will be provided with a list in advance of the dishes and a head count. You can budget staff hours, food costs, and figure your exact profit percentage based on the customer's advance order. You may even want to designate a staff member, such as an experienced hostess or server, as your banquet and catering coordinator.

Most restaurants with a successful catering side-business have at least one designated party planner on staff. You can pay her a higher hourly rate and your catering customers will have a regular staff member who they can contact when they want to schedule a private event. This is especially good for business customers—they like consistency when they place a catering or banquet order.

You will have many factors that affect your menu planning for special events. How many people will be served? Do the guests have special dietary needs? Do you have enough space, servers, and equipment for larger parties?

Your special menu needs to offer a variety of foods and a choice for low and high budget. Understand that different occasions are going to require different foods. For example, a wedding rehearsal dinner is going to be high-end steaks, chicken, or seafood items. They are going to expect great service and constant attention from servers and other staff. This will be a high-dollar event.

A child's birthday party, on the other hand, will generally be a hands-off affair with pizzas, pastas, and maybe some small desserts. You may have to have a server, or you may not.

Make sure all of your planned events are in writing. Point out any cancellation fees and have the customer initial them. Any changes to the original contract (number of guests, etc.) must also be confirmed in writing. Always negotiate food and beverage costs on a per-head basis. This will ensure that you are paid even if there are no-shows. This will save you from a nasty argument later.

Don't be afraid to say no to small parties. Find out what your minimum banquet price will be, and find a polite way to decline. You can also offer to take smaller private parties on slower days such as Mondays or Tuesdays.

There are a number of good books dedicated to the catering business, which is its own niche within the restaurant industry.

One of the best is Denise Vivaldo's; ***How to Start a Home-Based Catering Business. The Professional Caterer's Handbook*** by Lora Arduser is also good.

Private Banquets

If you have potential banquet space, you can tap into a great market by offering meeting facilities and special menus for parties such as birthdays, meetings, and other events.

The banquet event will consist of five stages:
1. Reservation, confirmation, and deposit

2. Preparation and room set-up
3. Service
4. Clean-up

Make sure that you have written guidelines for how your catering or special events are prearranged. Decide whether or not you are going to offer food, beverages, liquor, etc. Also decide if your restaurant is going to provide full service banquets, including flowers, music, and linen rentals.

Develop a brochure or an information packet that describes your menus and other amenities. Your catering and banquet menus will be smaller than your regular menu. Make sure that they are dishes that are quickly and easily produced in large volume, and are served easily. They must also be dishes that keep for longer periods.

You can offer your existing menu at different prices, such as family-style with much larger portions. A few chafing dishes and long tables can set your restaurant up for buffet dining and special events. If you have the space, it's a small investment for a big return.

If you decide to offer a buffet-style banquet, consider using a cook "helper" to dish out the customer portions. That way, you offer full-service, and this prevents gorging! Customers are often too embarrassed to go up and ask for third and fourth servings, and it drastically cuts food waste at a banquet. When guests serve themselves, they almost always throw away too much food.

This seems obvious, but you have to make sure your food is good and also right for your local customer base in order to be successful. Know your market! Not recognizing customers' needs is one of the main reasons why new restaurants fail—and this is something you can easily fix! As a chef, or restaurant owner, you MUST understand your customers' needs and wishes. You may personally love a dish, but if your sales mix shows poor sales, it's time to remove the item from your menu.

Customers, especially your regulars, want security—they want to be sure that they will get the same food and dining experience every time. Practice consistency in your dish preparation, plating techniques, and make sure you train all your staff so they know what your expectations are.

Your "signature dish" should always be an item that is highly popular with your guests, not something that you enjoy personally. Take your own tastes out of the equation. An easy way to do this is to ask your staff to rate their favorites. Do regular menu tastings and ask for feedback. Find out what your customers are thinking with feedback cards on every table.

Attend Local Special Events or Holidays

Does your city have a wine or food festival every year? How about a craft fair? Get a food booth and sell your food there! It's great advertising for your restaurant, and you still get to make money! Make sure you have plenty of menus, flyers, refrigerator magnets, etc. with your name and contact information on them. If your restaurant is a "theme restaurant," make sure you jazz up your booth with decorations. Dazzle your customers and sell, sell, sell!

Attending local events gets your name out in the community, and people like that. Customers enjoy seeing the chef "behind" the food.

Closing Thoughts

Restaurant competition is fierce. Running a kitchen is not for the faint of heart. Managing a thriving kitchen isn't just about fixing problems and putting together employee schedules. Successful chefs are also successful leaders.

Your restaurant will not survive if you can't learn how to follow a budget and still act like a role model for all your employees. Strong chefs understand that their success is not possible without the efforts of their crew. Results are achieved with people, and ultimately, the focus of your job will be on modifying employee behavior. There are profitable behaviors, and unprofitable behaviors—you must learn how to mediate and lead your employees both by example and by teaching.

Prepare yourself by balancing the needs of your employees with the needs of your restaurant. A profitable kitchen must do both. Solving problems will always be a part of your job. But you can be prepared for most obstacles just by approaching you position objectively and learning as much as you can about the industry you have chosen.

Your passion and dedication to your position and your staff will be the main component of you eventual success. Stay focused, committed, and alert to opportunities. True dedication will pay off in dollars!

About the Author

With over twenty years in the restaurant industry, and over a decade as an executive trainer and Executive Chef, J.A. Mendez has traveled all over the United States, training new chefs, opening new restaurants, and helping to revive struggling restaurants from the brink of disaster. He is a professional member of the American Culinary Federation.

Note: The author has no financial interest in and receives no compensation from manufacturers of products or websites mentioned in this book.

Important Resources for Chefs

American Association of Franchisees & Dealers (AAFD)
www.aafd.org

American Culinary Federation
www.acfchefs.org

American Dietetic Association (ADA)
www.eatright.org

American Franchisee Association (AFA)
www.franchisee.org

American Hotel & Lodging Assoc. Educational Institute
www.ei-ahla.org

American Institute of Baking
www.aibonline.org

American Institute of Wine and Food
www.aiwf.org

American Meat Science Association
www.meatscience.org

American Personal & Private Chef Association
www.personalchef.com

American Society for Healthcare Food Service Administrators
www.ashfsa.org

Association of Correctional Food Service Affiliates (ACFSA)
www.acfsa.org

Chef's Collaborative
www.chefscollaborative.org

Chef's Commandments Website
www.thechefscommandments.com

Club Managers Association of America (CMAA)
www.cmaa.org

Commercial Food Equipment Service Association
www.cfesa.com

Council of Hotel and Restaurant Trainers (CHART)
www.chart.org

Council of International Restaurant Real Estate Brokers
www.cirb.net

Council on Hotel, Restaurant, and Institutional Education
www.chrie.org

Dietary Managers Association (DMA)
www.dmaonline.org

Epicurious
www.epicurious.com

Food and Wine Magazine
www.foodandwine.com

Food Network

www.foodnetwork.com

Foodservice Consultants Society International (FCSI)
www.fcsi.org

Foodservice Word (Kostuch Publications) Limited)
www.foodserviceworld.com

Hospitality Financial & Technology Professional
swww.hftp.org

Institute of Food Technologists
www.ift.org

International Association in Food Protection
www.foodprotection.org

International Association of Culinary Professionals (IACP)
www.iacp.com

International Dairy-Deli-Bakery Association
www.iddba.org

International Food, Wine & Travel Writers Association
www.ifwtwa.org

International Foodservice Distributors Association (IFDA)
www.ifdaonline.org

International Foodservice Editorial Council
www.ifeconline.com

International Franchise Association (IFA)
www.franchise.org

International Hotel & Restaurant Association (IH&RA)
www.ih-ra.com

James Beard Foundation
www.jamesbeard.org

Les Dames d'Escoffier
www.ldei.org

Manufacturers Agents Association for the Foodservice Industry (MAFSI)
www.mafsi.org

Multicultural Foodservice & Hospitality Alliance (MFHA)
www.mfha.net

National Restaurant Association
www.restaurant.org

Nation's Restaurant News
www.nrn.com

National Association of Catering Executives
www.nace.net

National Association of College & University Food Services
www.nacufs.org

National Association of Concessionaires
www.naconline.org

National Bartender's Organization
www.bartender.org

National Club Association
www.nationalclub.org

National Restaurant Association
www.restaurant.org

National Society of Minorities in Hospitality
www.nsmh.org

North American Association of Food Equipment Manufacturers (NAFEM)
www.nafem.org

School Nutrition Association
www.asfsa.org

Share Our Strength
www.strength.org

Slow Food International
www.slowfood.com

StarChefs
www.starchefs.com

United States Personal Chef Association
www.uspca.com

Women Chefs & Restaurateurs
www.womenchefs.org

Women's Foodservice Forum
www.womensfoodserviceforum.com

Proud Member of SPAWN

Small publishers, Artists, and Writers Network

www.spawn.org

Helpful Companies and Contributors

This is for informational use only. The author and the publisher have no financial interest in and receive no compensation from manufacturers of products or websites mentioned in this book. No information contained in this book should be considered as financial, tax, or legal advice. Your reliance upon information and content obtained by you at or through this publication is solely at your own risk.

Detex Alarms
Detex Corporation
302 Detex Drive
New Braunfels, Texas 78130
800-729-3839
www.detex.com
sales@detex.com

Ecolab Food Safety Solutions
Food Safety Specialties Inc.
(Formerly Daydots)
1801 Riverbend West Drive
Fort Worth, Texas 76118-7031

https://www.daydots.com
http://www.ecolab.com

O'Dell Restaurant Consulting
Brandon O'Dell
blog.bodellconsulting.com
brandon@bodellconsulting.com
Office: (888) 571-9068
www.bodellconsulting.com

Softcafé
Menu Design Software
Restaurant Menu Design, Menu Printing, and Employee Scheduling Software from Softcafé.
www.softcafe.com

Collette Szymborski, CPA
Certified Public Accountant
Managing Partner
Elk Grove Accountancy Corporation
9401 E. Stockton Blvd, Suite 115
Elk Grove, California 95624

Send us your stories!

We'd love to hear your input, and your restaurant tips and stories. We might even include your story in the next edition of our book. If we do include your story, we will send you $50!

Mailing address:
Pineapple Publications
ATTN: Chef's Commandments
PO Box 580465
Elk Grove, CA 95758

You can also submit your story at:

www.thechefscommandments.com

Index

Corporate Orders

Would you like to order The Chef's Commandments series for your next manager's training exercise? The Chef's Commandments also makes a wonderful corporate gift, and can be specially ordered for your next company holiday party or employee event.

Corporate volume discounts:

Number of Copies	Price per copy
1-20 copies: List Price	$15.95
21-50 copies: 10% discount off list price	$14.35
51-100 copies 20% discount off list price	$12.96
101-1,000 copies 30% discount off list price	$11.16
1,001-5,000 copies 40% discount off list price	$9.57
5,001-10,000 copies 45% discount off the list price	$8.77

More than 10,000 copies, please contact us at
http://www.thechefscommandments.com/contact-us.html

Order Form

Name____
Company____
Address ____
City, State, Zip ______________________________________
Telephone ____
Website ____

Number of books ____________ X ea. Price ___________ = ______
Please add 7.75% for sales in California

Mail your order form with a check or money order to: **Pineapple Publications, PO Box 580465, Elk Grove, CA 95758**

8943749R0

Made in the USA
Lexington, KY
16 March 2011